How to Control Your

Anger

Before It Controls You

How to Control Your
Anger
Before It Controls You

Albert Ellis, Ph.D.
and
Raymond Chip Tafrate, Ph.D.

Citadel Press
Kensington Publishing Corp.
www.kensingtonbooks.com

CITADEL PRESS books are published by

Kensington Publishing Corp.
850 Third Avenue
New York, NY 10022

Copyright © 1997 Albert Ellis Institute

All Kensington titles, imprints, and distributed lines are available at special
quantity discounts for bulk purchases for sales promotions, premiums,
fund raising, educational, or institutional use. Special book excerpts or
customized printings can also be created to fit specific needs. For details,
write or phone the office of the Kensington special sales manager:
Kensington Publishing Corp., 850 Third Avenue, New York, NY 10022,
attn: Special Sales Department, phone 1-800-221-2647.

Kensington and the K logo Reg. U.S. Pat. & TM Office
Citadel Press is a trademark of Kensington Publishing Corp.

First printing 1998

20 19 18 17 16 15 14 13 12

Printed in the United States of America

Library of Congress Cataloging-in-Publication Data

Ellis, Albert.
    How to control your anger—before it controls you / Albert Ellis –
Raymond Chip Tafrate.
        p. cm.
    "A Citadel Press book."
    Includes bibliographical references and index.
    ISBN 0-8065-2010-8 (pbk.)
    1. Anger.   I. Tafrate, Raymond Chip.   II. Title.
BF575.A5E435   1997
152.47—dc21   95-15779
                                                CIP

For Janet and Lauren
With Love

"What disturbs people's minds is not events but their judgments on events."

Epictetus, First Century A.D.

Contents

Preface: Can You Unangrily Deal With Your Anger?   ix

1. The Grim Costs of Anger   3
2. Myths About How to Deal With Your Anger   18
3. REBT and the ABC's of Anger   27
4. Rational and Irrational Aspects of Anger   33
5. Discovering Your Rage-Creating Beliefs   39
6. Special Insights Into Your Self-Angering Beliefs   47
7. Disputing Your Self-Angering Beliefs   51
8. More Ways of Thinking Yourself Out of Your Anger   56
9. Feeling Your Way Out of Your Anger   62
10. Acting Your Way Out of Your Anger   72
11. Learning to Relax   92
12. Still More Ways of Thinking Yourself Out of Your   103
    Anger
13. Additional Ways of Reducing Your Anger   124
14. Accepting Yourself With Your Anger   144
15. A Few Concluding Remarks   151

Appendix: REBT Self-Help Form   153
Selected References   159
Index   175

Preface

Can You Unangrily Deal With Your Anger?

YOU DON'T HAVE TO LOOK VERY FAR to witness the destructive impact anger can have on human lives. Just turn on the television or read a newspaper and you will undoubtedly notice that anger plays a role in all sorts of atrocities large and small. Anger can have equally disastrous effects on your own life. Left unchecked, it can destroy some of your closest relationships and undermine your physical and mental health.

It seems to be one of the great paradoxes of psychotherapy that while anger can be one of the most destructive emotions, it is also the one that people seem most confused about and choose to work on the least.

Although numerous books and magazines tell us how to deal with anger, none of the advice seems to work that well. And with what contradictions! Some advise you to take a passive, nonresistant attitude when others treat you shabbily. That presumably shows everyone that you are in real control of yourself. Firm and strong. But passive acceptance often leads to continued unfairness. Worse yet, it may even heighten it.

Other books on anger cavalierly push you to freely and fully express your enraged feelings. Vent them assertively. Let them all hang out. Be your honest raging self. That will fix your opponents!

Maybe it will. But as love begets love, rage begets reprisals. Try it and see!

Because both of these approaches to anger produce dubious results, what's the solution? Carefully bottle up your fury, or carelessly express it? Quite a question!

The solution? Epictetus, a remarkably wise stoic philosopher, pointed out some two thousand years ago that you choose to overreact to the obnoxious and unfair behavior of others. You don't have to. And, as he did, you can more wisely choose to react much differently. That is one of the main teachings of Rational Emotive Behavior Therapy (REBT), which follows the age-old wisdom of several Asian and European philosophers and combines it with some of the most modern methods of psychotherapy. You can use REBT methods to greatly reduce your self-defeating, angry reactions and to live unhysterically in an often difficult and unfair world.

Can you do this by yourself? Yes, you definitely can make significant changes in how you live with and handle your anger. The good news is that with some effort, you can learn to overcome your ranting and raging. Both authors of this book have devoted much of their professional careers to understanding and helping people who suffer from severe hostility. We will now share with you some of the methods we have found to be effective for many of our clients who have sought help for their anger.

Since publishing the first version of this book over two decades ago I (AE) have received thousands of endorsements from people who have benefited from applying REBT principles to their anger problems. Although there are a number of new chapters and changes in this current edition, which reflect exciting advancements made in the understanding of anger, many of the basic principles outlined in the first edition remain as effective today as they were over two decades ago. So once again, in this revised and updated edition, I and my able collaborator, Dr. Raymond Chip Tafrate, will explain exactly how you create your own philosophy of anger by consciously and unconsciously resorting to absolutist, dictatorial thinking. We will show you how, by changing your enraged thoughts, feelings, and behaviors, you can minimize your anger and live a happier and more effective life.

How to Control Your

Anger

Before It Controls You

1

The Grim Costs of Anger

YOU ARE PROBABLY READING THIS BOOK because either you or someone you care about has a problem with anger. Before we begin to show you and your loved ones how to reduce anger, let us briefly look at some of its grim costs.

Why should you and those you care about work to push away your honest and heartfelt feelings of rage? Obviously, there is no law of the universe that says you absolutely must do so. But there are some important reasons why you'd darned well better.

ANGER DESTROYS PERSONAL RELATIONSHIPS

Damage to personal relationships is one of the most common costs of anger, and probably the worst. The relationships that are damaged are often your best. You may believe, like many people do, that anger is something we direct mostly at people we dislike. Wrong! Several recent surveys conducted by psychologists, one at Hofstra University (Kassinove et al.) and the other at the University of Massachusetts (Averill), tell us this is not true. We more commonly make ourselves angry at individuals we know well. The most frequent targets of anger include spouses, children, coworkers, and friends. The following case examples illustrate this point.

Jeff was in his late fifties when he came into therapy to get control over his explosive temper. He was divorced with two grown children. He said that his wife became fed up with his angry outbursts and controlling behaviors and had divorced him several years before. Even when he still had some contact with his children, their relationship was often strained. Once, while visiting with his daughter, he got into an argument with his son-in-law. The exchange became so heated that Jeff actually punched him. Since that time both his children had refused to have any contact with him. When looking back, Jeff sadly realized that his anger had contributed to the loss of most of his close family ties.

Nancy was twenty-six years old when she sought help. At that time she had been living with her boyfriend, Fred, for about two years. They had been planning to get married, but Nancy's anger at Fred was destroying their relationship. She reported feeling jealous and enraged about him working closely with other women and complained that he was not paying enough attention to her. While there was no evidence that Fred was romantically involved with any of his coworkers, Nancy would search for things he was doing wrong. Periodically she would accuse him of all sorts of horrors and sometimes yell and throw things around the house. Fred finally got fed up with her angry displays, broke off the engagement, and moved out.

These two cases may seem somewhat extreme but actually are not that unusual. People like Jeff will frequently put the blame on others when their relationships are rough. They refuse to compromise or adjust when disagreements arise. It's not until some of their relationships begin falling apart that they take some responsibility for their anger and really notice its grim costs. In many cases, they don't realize that their own angry feelings and outbursts have led them to lose friends and fail to influence people—until it's much too late!

Nancy's case was a little different. The loss of just one important relationship was enough for her to see that she had a problem with anger control. But at first, even she blamed her rage on her ex-fiancé. She reasoned that because she was feeling so hurt and angry, Fred must be wrong. She didn't improve until she accepted responsibility for her own lack of emotional control.

Think about your own life. Has your anger ruined any important relationships? Do you tend to blame other people for how you are feeling? If you continue this pattern, where will you be a few years from now? Letting go of your anger and being more accepting and flexible in close relationships will probably serve you better in the long—and short—run.

ANGER DISRUPTS WORK RELATIONSHIPS

Let's face it, work is often very frustrating. Demanding bosses, jealous coworkers, irate customers, deadlines, unfairness of all sorts—these can all test your patience. Your anger about frustrations, however, can frustrate you more. First, it can ruin work relationships and impede your success. Second, it can block your focusing on important issues and limit your ability to do quality work.

Getting along with other people helps you succeed on the job and may even be as important as your ability to do the job itself. Coworkers and supervisors hate working with you if you have temper outbursts. They will see you as a difficult customer and want to run for the nearest exit. A study conducted by the Center for Creative Leadership in North Carolina found that among executives, the inability to handle anger, especially in pressure situations, was a major factor in missing promotions, being fired, or being asked to retire.

And not only among executives! Hostility can sabotage you in all sorts of work settings and at different employment levels. Let's look at two very different case examples:

Jerry, a construction worker, started therapy because he was afraid his angry outbursts might lose him his job. Although he was physically capable of handling his work, Jerry was short in stature. He would often get teased by his coworkers about his height. In response to these insults, Jerry became visibly enraged. This led to even more ridicule. At one point, Jerry became so angry that he actually threatened to assault another employee. He was suspended and told that if he lost his temper on the job once again he would be fired.

Fortunately, Jerry used REBT methods to reduce his angry feelings first, and then was able to respond more effectively to people's ridicule. Let's look at another case:

Howard was the owner of a small accounting agency. His business consisted of himself and an administrative assistant. Howard was feeling depressed because his business was not doing very well—especially because, over the past year, he had lost five different assistants. Important work was not getting done and he had to constantly keep retraining somebody new. Howard overreacted strongly to any sort of frustration, screaming, banging on the furniture, and even breaking the phone on several occasions. He foolishly figured that he had every right to be angry because it was his business and he was paying the salary of his assistant. A few REBT sessions helped him to realize that his angry outbursts were driving people away and proving to be very costly.

In both of these cases, angry feelings and outbursts were destroying important work relationships. Jerry needed the support of his coworkers and supervisors to keep his job and to move upward. Howard mistakenly assumed that just because he was the boss everyone would have to accept his temper tantrums.

Being able to manage your emotions on the job, in spite of inevitable frustrations, is often crucial in building a successful career. Giving vent to your anger often feels great to you—but hardly to your business or professional associates!

Anger also diverts your energy and attention away from your work. How? By driving you to ruminate about some "unfair" situation, and to run it uselessly over and over in your head. Or by your obsessing about seeking revenge against a coworker or supervisor. Or by pushing you to engage in subtle sabotage, to refuse to follow sensible directions, to let important things slide, or even to go out of your way to destroy someone else's work.

How will your madly focusing on some "unjust" person, or on plotting and scheming revenge, help you constructively resolve conflicts or do quality work? Badly! Your rage, over time, will certainly be noticed by people around you. Observe the case of Jane:

> Jane came into treatment because she could not stop ruminating about why she did not get a recent promotion. She had been with her company for over five years and expected to be promoted to a managerial position. When this did not happen she felt hurt and enraged. The more she thought about it, the more angry she made herself. While Jane masked her anger from her boss, her enthusiasm for her work declined, her performance waned, and she failed to follow through on several projects. After a month of this, Jane's boss called her in to his office, expressed his concern, and revealed that her failing to get a promotion had more to do with budget problems than her job performance. He reassured her that she was the next in line for a promotion—however, if she did not get back to being more productive, the firm would promote someone else.

Jane had spent so much time and energy inwardly raging at her boss that she never stopped to think of other reasons why she did not get promoted. So she acted in a manner that decreased her chances of getting the raise. Result: She almost ruined her chances for advancement.

You may, of course, sometimes find yourself in work situations that are indeed unfair and unrewarding. But by reacting angrily or by impulsively "running away," you encourage people to conclude that you cannot handle frustration and are likely to enrage yourself when things get tough again. A much better alternative is to reduce your anger and do your best to improve the situation. If this does not work, you may unangrily decide to move on and seek a more rewarding work environment.

MAKING DIFFICULT SITUATIONS WORSE

In spite of what we have just said, doesn't anger have some gains? Doesn't feeling angry sometimes help you to face difficult situations? Won't it help you to feel empowered and in control when confronted with adversity? Isn't expressing your anger necessary for asserting yourself and getting your points across? Good questions. Psychological research has not yet definitively shown whether anger increases or decreases your effectiveness in handling difficulties. In fact, few researchers have even bothered to look at this issue. Nonetheless, many people, including some therapists and popular writers, have jumped to the conclusion that you must feel angry when facing unfair situations.

A somewhat different perspective emerged over two thousand years ago from some of the Asian and Greek and Roman philosophers. In one of the earliest essays on anger, the Stoic philosopher Seneca described anger as "the most hideous and frenzied of all the emotions." The Stoics observed that anger has the capacity to cloud people's ability to reason effectively.

Among the numerous clients we have seen with anger problems, many are quite intelligent and have good skills for resolving conflict and difficulties—when they are not enraged. After they have cooled down, they can calmly identify different ways they could have better handled troublesome situations.

Try to remember the last time you felt extremely angry. Recall what you focused upon and how you acted. Were you able to reasonably consider good courses of action? Were you able to look at all your options? Did you make the best decision? Do you regret something you said or did? If you are like most people, you will see that you hardly think and behave at your best when you feel enraged.

Also observe how other people act when they are very angry. Look at your relatives, friends, and coworkers. Or just turn on your television set. News broadcasts and talk shows are full of examples. During a tough interview, how effective are people who lose their cool? Does anger help debaters make their points logically and reasonably?

But, you may ask, what about situations where someone is fighting against some form of injustice or unfairness? What about struggling for large-scale social reforms, such as equal rights? Isn't anger appropriate and effective in these situations?

While anger may help in some situations, it rarely aids sensible change. Leaders such as Martin Luther King Jr., Mahatma Gandhi, and others were forcefully committed to and passionate about their causes. But they were also extremely disciplined and clear-headed. They were effective because they mainly relied on reason and not on anger.

We all struggle at times. Life is difficult and challenging. While anger is a natural human emotion, it is hardly the most useful for solving problems. Think about it—and decide whether rage is helpful or hurtful for you.

ANGER SPARKS AGGRESSION

Another reason to curb anger is that it can easily lead to aggression. Haven't you witnessed violence in your own life? And on the screen and in the news? Isn't our own American culture one of the most violent of any industrialized country?

According to recent statistics of the Federal Bureau of Investigation, one violent crime occurs in the United States every seventeen seconds (U.S. Department of Justice). Acts of brute force are especially prevalent among our nation's youth. Homicide is currently the second leading cause of death among fifteen-to-twenty-four-year-olds, making interpersonal violence one of the most important public heath problems (U.S. Bureau of the Census).

So is family violence. It is estimated that in the United States about a million and a half women are battered by their partners each year. Approximately 40 percent of all the women who are murdered in this country every year die at the hands of their husbands. Not that women are themselves exempt from acting violently. A recent survey showed that women assaulted men more often than the reverse. Be cautious, however, about such comparisons, because when men assault women the consequences tend to be more severe (Straus and Gelles).

Violence in families also takes a grim toll on young children. A government report concluded that in the United States approximately 140,000 children a year suffer serious injury from child abuse. At least two thousand children a year—more than five each day—die at the hands of their parents or caretakers (U.S. Advisory Board on Child Abuse and Neglect).

While anger does not automatically lead to aggression, it can often do so. As one anger investigator put it, "Anger can be likened to an architect's blueprint. The availability of a blueprint does not cause a building to be constructed, but it does make construction easier."

The cost of anger as an instigator of aggression is illustrated in the following two case examples:

Rich was a thirty-seven-year-old husband who started treatment after his arrest for assault and battery. His wife had long complained about his aggressive behavior while driving. She insisted that he get help when another driver cut Rich off at a traffic light, almost causing an accident. Rich enraged himself and followed the driver to the next light. He then got out of his car and exchanged words with the other angry driver. Rich punched him in the face and then left the scene. Police later caught up with him after a witness provided his license plate number. When seen for therapy, Rich revealed that he got angry and exchanged words with other drivers at least once a month. This had resulted in other fights, though this was the first time he had been arrested.

Shirley was in her early thirties when she sought help for constantly screaming at her three young children. She reported that her kids continually frustrated her, that she received little help from her husband, and that she felt that she never had a minute for herself. Her outbursts were getting worse and she was breaking objects around the house. She was worried that she might be harming her children psychologically and feared losing control and hurting them physically.

Like Rich and Shirley, a number of people seek help for their anger because it often leads to violent behaviors. Costs associated with aggression include loss of relationships, loss of jobs, physical injury, damaged property, lawsuits, jail sentences, and feelings of guilt and embarrassment.

Try to remember the last time you were aggressive. Think of times when you may have destroyed property, yelled, screamed, pushed, slapped, or punched somebody. Weren't you—honestly?—impelled by some degree of anger? Even rare expressions of violence can be costly. If you get enraged frequently, watch it!

ANGER MAY LEAD TO HEART DISEASE

Maybe you are thinking to yourself, "I'm perfectly healthy and this section doesn't really apply to me." Don't be so sure! Over thirty years of research shows how chronic anger and the development of heart disease are often connected. Heart disease is currently the leading cause of death among Americans. While your anger may not as yet have produced serious health problems, its damaging effects may already be at work.

To understand how anger can harm your body, let us review its purpose and function. Many researchers view anger as an emotional system that prepares and energizes us for action against a potential source of threat and that assists us in mobilizing our resources to deal with conflict. Early in this century this type of emergency response was studied by the physiologist Walter Cannon, who coined the term the "fight or flight" response. The flight part of the response goes with anxiety and fleeing from a dangerous situation. The fight portion goes more with anger and defending yourself against some kind of threat.

What happens in your body when you feel angry and your emergency response gets going? Physical changes, such as increases in muscle tension, heart rate, breathing, and metabolism, help ready your body for action. Also, adrenaline pours into your bloodstream and your blood flows to the larger muscles in your body. It is not surprising that people often report the urge to strike out at the target of their anger. Their bodies are prepared to do just that.

Anger, therefore, can help you confront a life-threatening attacker or some other real emergency. But it does not make much sense when you are responding to some of the usual frustrations of everyday life. In fact, if you keep activating your anger-creating system, it can take a serious toll on your body.

Robert Sapolsky, a professor of biology and neuroscience at Stanford University, has described how, when we repeatedly bring on the physical changes that go with rage, we can damage our cardiovascular systems. Sudden increases in blood pressure that accompany our anger increase the force at which blood moves through our arteries. These surges in blood flow can wear down and damage the smooth lining of these arteries, causing them to become scarred or pitted. Once this layer of tissue becomes damaged, fatty acids, glucose, and other material from the blood begin to stick to the damaged walls of these vessels. The accumulation of these materials over time can eventually lead to a clogging of the arteries, which in turn results in an overall decrease in blood flow. This condition is known as atherosclerosis. If this buildup of material, also known as plaque, occurs in the arteries going to your heart you may be a candidate for coronary heart disease, myocardial ischemia, or a variety of other serious heart ailments.

Since the early 1960s there have been a number of important studies showing a relationship between anger and heart disease. A complete review of this research is beyond the scope of this book. Generally, most of the studies tend to fall into two main categories. In the first category, known as cross-sectional research, groups of patients with heart disease are asked to report the frequency and intensity of anger they routinely experience. Their responses are then compared to a matched group of individuals, called control subjects, who do not suffer from heart disease. In the overwhelming majority of these studies, individuals who suffer from coronary artery disease report significantly higher levels of anger than individuals who do not have heart disease. The implication is that people who experience higher levels of anger are more likely to have a problem with heart disease.

Another group of studies tells us even more about the cause and effect relationship between anger and heart disease. In these prospective studies, a large group of initially healthy people are asked to answer questions about the levels of anger that they experience in their lives. They are then followed over long periods of time, twenty years or more in some cases, at the end of which they are examined for heart disease. The original anger and hostility scores are then checked and matched to each individual's physical health status. In the majority of these studies, a high degree of anger or hostility actually predicted the later development of atherosclerosis.

For example, in one study, 255 medical students filled out a personality questionnaire. In the follow-up twenty-five years later it was found that those who scored high on a measure of hostility had four to five times the rate of coronary heart disease than subjects who scored lower on this measure. In a similar study conducted with lawyers, nearly one in five who had scored in the top quarter for hostility was dead by the age of fifty. Among those lawyers who scored in the lowest quarter, only one in twenty-five had died.

So how long have you been fairly angry? Are you a candidate for high blood pressure or even a heart attack? If you chronically experience anger you may be increasing your risk for serious illness later on in life. The next time you feel angry, try to become aware of some of the physical sensations and changes that are occurring in your body. Remember that physical reactions accompanying your chronic anger can lead to damage, illness, and possibly premature death.

ANGER AND PERSONAL DISTRESS

Many of the costs of anger are very dramatic and noticeable. Other costs, however, may be less obvious. These include serious emotional and personal distress, such as depression, guilt, embarrassment, feeling out of control, and lack of confidence in dealing with other people. Do you have such feelings along with your low frustration tolerance and rage?

As we have been noting, intense and frequent anger often causes you to lose jobs and important relationships. When your rage leads to such losses, you can easily put yourself down and make yourself feel depressed. Anger and depression can sometimes afflict you simultaneously. Thus, you may blame other people and things and make yourself angry—and also you may beat up on yourself and bring on depression. This was the case with Stacy:

> Stacy was in her late thirties and had three young children. When she came into therapy, she reported feeling sad and lonely and complained that she was not getting any support from the people around her. She admitted that she was not content being a housewife. In fact, she was quite angry about not being able to pursue some of her life's dreams. Her husband was putting in long hours at work and did not seem interested in spending time with her. Stacy's parents, who lived nearby, preferred spending more time with their other daughter and her family. In addition, Stacy had few close friends.

Stacy's case is interesting because her primary problem may have been more related to anger than depression. Her depressed and hostile attitude made it difficult for others to be around her. At times she would blame other people for her predicament, such as her husband, her children, and her family. Then she would feel extremely angry. Stacy truly desired to be close to others, but her anger was driving them away.

At other times, Stacy would blame herself for her loneliness and pictured a life without any friendships and with unfulfilled ambitions. She then experienced sadness and depression. Thus, Stacy would seesaw between feelings of anger and depression. Unfortunately, neither of these disturbed feelings was helping her create the kind of life she wanted. In fact, her rage led to greater loss of intimacy and to her feeling more lonely and depressed.

If you feel depression about your own anger, you can break this connection by letting go of your anger and focusing on changing those things in your life that are not working.

As with depression, guilt and embarrassment may also follow your frequent rages. Thus, you may feel so embarrassed about things you have said or done when angry that you put yourself down and avoid people with whom you are upset. This happened with Bob:

> Bob had a long history of problems with his temper. At a supermarket, he got into a fight with the store manager over the price of some items. Since the store manager was much younger than he, Bob believed that he should have been shown more respect. When this did not happen, Bob made himself enraged. After Bob repeatedly cursed and threatened the manager, the police were finally called. Bob became even more enraged and had to be subdued and led away in handcuffs. Although the charges were dropped, Bob continued to avoid the supermarket and any people who knew about the incident because he felt so ashamed of his behavior.

While Bob's case is extreme, guilt and embarrassment about your own fury can easily lead to your withdrawal from others. This will continue to disrupt your personal relationships and will block your growth.

Rage may also make you feel out of control. When your heart begins to pound, your face gets hot, your thoughts race, your blood pressure skyrockets, and adrenaline surges through your body, you will seldom act in a rational way. Your rage may lead to a constant struggle to control your actions. Your fury itself may feel very uncomfortable and be a constant reminder that you are not dealing effectively with the world around you.

> Mike was twenty-nine years old when he sought help with his anger. He described himself as a "react-a-holic" and reported many incidents where he had flown off the handle and acted aggressively. Since high school, he had lost important relationships, been arrested once for assault, and been fired from several jobs due to his angry outbursts. At the time Mike came for

REBT he had been married three years, and his wife had recently borne a son. The birth motivated him to get help. He wanted better control over his emotions and said, "I don't want to be angry around my kid."

Like Mike, do you worry about going too far when you are angry? Are you afraid that you may lose control and act destructively? Feeling out of control can be a signal that it's time to get help.

Anger may also make you lose confidence about dealing with others. If your rage often brings you poor results, you may soon begin to question your own judgment. You may stop being assertive for fear of acting angrily and going too far. You may feel confused about how to respond to everyday difficulties. Learning how to manage your emotions when faced with problems certainly helps.

Letting go of your anger does not mean forfeiting your dreams and desires. Quite the contrary! By minimizing your anger you will tend to act confidently and assertively, thus increasing your chances of getting what you want out of life.

While many of the costs of rage are dramatic and easily observable by others, some are privately experienced and lead to embarrassment, lack of control, confusion, and lack of confidence. You can also make yourself depressed and guilty about feeling angry by bringing on real disadvantages. Three bad feelings for the price of one!

ARE YOU SUFFERING THE COSTS OF ANGER?

Do any of the scenarios in this section sound familiar to you? Is anger helping you to get what you want out of life? Are its costs worth its pleasures? If you have not yet experienced the kinds of losses we have just described, keep in mind that rage does not always lead to noticeable damage right away. It can often take several years before it brings about serious consequences. If you have suffered from or are now risking setbacks from anger, isn't it time to get a handle on this problem?

Change is often difficult. The skills and techniques outlined in this book are not meant to be a quick and cheap solution to your problems. They require an open mind, a lot of practice, and constant effort in fighting against old angry patterns. Then it gets easier.

Deciding to live your life with less anger may be one of the most important decisions you will ever make. Well?

2

Myths About How to Deal With Your Anger

YOU HAVE NO DOUBT HEARD many "commonsense" suggestions for dealing with your anger. Popular magazines, television talk shows, and radio-talk show hosts daily offer solutions that are supposed to help you live a life free of anger and resentment. Unfortunately, many of these ideas simply don't work.

If you consulted today with five different mental health professionals about how to best deal with your anger, you would probably get five different methods of treatment. Some "experts" will tell you that the solution to your anger problem lies in your past. The only way to successfully deal with your rage is to go back and heal old wounds and injustices that have made you into an insecure and angry individual. Others, however, may advise you that your past doesn't count. If you change your present job, relationships, or situations that upset you, then you will undoubtedly lead a happier, healthier, less angry life.

You may get other conflicting views about what to do with your anger. Some professionals will recommend that you hold it in and wherever possible avoid conflict with troublesome people. You may be told to remove yourself from difficult situations and not to return until you have cooled down. Opposing this line of reasoning, you may be encouraged to let your anger out whenever you feel it. You can do this by openly expressing yourself to rotten people. Or you can indirectly let your anger out by privately screaming, beating on pillows, or engaging in physical exercise.

Misconceptions about anger prevail. Why? Because there has been a lack of good scientific investigation into the causes of and solutions to anger problems. As psychiatrist Allen Rothenberg says, "Almost invariably, anger has not been considered an independent topic worthy of investigation....[This] has not only deprived anger of its rightful importance in the understanding of human behavior, but has also led to a morass of confused definitions, misconceptions, and simplistic theories."

Here are five common myths about how to deal with resentment and rage. To understand the real nature of anger, consider these myths and skeptically challenge them.

MYTH NO. 1: ACTIVELY EXPRESSING YOUR ANGER REDUCES IT

The view that you must actively express anger to reduce it stems from Freudian thinking. According to Freud's (and Wilhelm Reich's) hydraulic model of emotions, your angry feelings build up over time and create a reservoir of negative energy. If you do not express or release this pent-up rage it eventually bursts out in physical outbreaks, illness, and emotional disturbances. Therapists who subscribe to this theory encourage you to ventilate your angry feelings and thereby drain off your reservoir of pent-up tension. By forcefully telling nasty people off, or performing other cathartic acts, you will supposedly stop your aggressive energy from building to harmful levels.

This myth involves two important errors: first, that expressing your rage reduces its risks to your health; second, that letting your resentment out will make you feel less angry.

As we noted in chapter 1, there is a good deal of evidence that chronic anger is indeed a risk factor for heart disease. There are some studies that show a link between suppressed anger and illness. But are people who let their anger out really that much better off than people who don't?

Definitely not! According to Dr. Aaron Siegman, a psychologist and anger researcher at the University of Maryland, venting your anger is a serious risk factor for heart disease. Expressing rage may trigger the kind of internal arousal that is most likely to lead to artery damage. Dr. Siegman's research indicates that actively releasing anger is far more likely to be damaging to your health than holding your anger in. Blurting out your fury is quite risky!

What about the myth that people who express their anger openly and freely become less anger-prone? *Does* engaging in catharsis lead to reduced rage? A number of psychological experiments have examined this issue during the last forty years. These studies have consistently concluded that both verbal and physical expressions of anger lead to *more*, not less, anger and violence.

Letting your anger out directly and indirectly tends to reinforce and strengthen it. A colleague of ours who works with angry clients often tells this old joke, "How do you get to Carnegie Hall?" Answer: "Practice, practice, practice." So, "How do you become a really angry person?" Answer: "Practice, practice, practice."

If venting wrath usually leads to increased anger, why does the contrary myth still persist? One answer may have something to do with the nature of anger itself. As discussed in chapter 1, anger is a system that helps to prepare your body for action against a potential threat. When the physical changes that are part of this system occur, your body is charged up and ready to take some kind of action. It feels natural to strike out in some way. You may even feel some relief immediately after you engage in violence or tell someone off. Because giving vent to your anger may *feel* good, you are more likely to do it again and foolishly believe this is the healthy thing to do.

Another reason this myth persists is that most therapists genuinely want to help their clients feel and function better. Because clients may feel some temporary relief after venting their rage, many therapists also mistakenly believe that they are doing something helpful by encouraging them to blow off steam. In addition, therapists want to support their clients. After listening to them describe their outrage over an unjust incident, the therapist may think is right or proper for these clients to express their feelings.

Advising them to openly show their rage may indicate that the therapist really understands and cares.

In spite of the evidence, venting fury is still encouraged in many forms of psychotherapy and in our culture at large. If you still believe that letting your anger out is the healthy and productive thing to do, then you'd better rethink this outdated idea. Start by not giving in to those impulses to act on your anger. Try holding it in next time. You will see that eventually your agitation and arousal will simmer down. Then read on to learn how to stop yourself from getting into the vicious anger cycle to begin with.

MYTH NO. 2: TAKE TIME OUT
WHEN YOU FEEL ANGRY

Some mental health professionals who realize the dangers and costs of venting rage tell you to vigorously try to avoid or escape from those situations where you are likely to get angry. They call this procedure "time-out." This means that if you find yourself becoming angry with your kids, take a break. If your temper is rising at work, go for a walk until you calm down. Sounds like good advice, right? Well maybe not. There are some problems with this way of dealing with your anger. Let's look at two people who used this approach.

Fred had a history of becoming frustrated and nasty toward his women friends. While he never actually assaulted them, he would yell and scream and sometimes break objects when he lost his temper. After the loss of several relationships Fred sought help. His therapist at that time recommended that when he felt himself becoming angry he take a time-out. Fred tried this approach in his next relationship, and it seemed to work well for a couple of months. His new partner, however, also eventually left. She complained that Fred did not communicate with her and that they could rarely work out disagreements because he would always run away.

Marjorie was also practicing the time-out strategy. She used it mostly at work when she felt overwhelmed by the demands of her customers and supervisors. While she did not have any temper outbursts, her avoiding technique was noticed by people around her. She developed the reputation of being emotionally fragile. Supervisors and coworkers held back from giving Marjorie any kind of challenging work for fear she could not handle it. Eventually she was let go from her job because her manager did not believe she could deal with its pressures.

Both Fred and Marjorie were actively practicing avoidance. In Fred's case he avoided any kind of disagreement—but also evaded the communication required to sustain an intimate relationship. Marjorie avoided anything at work that she believed would add to her agitation, and therefore could not perform her job well.

Given enough time, avoidance usually backfires. This happens for two reasons. First, you are not addressing problems that had better be solved. When you run away from difficulties they do not magically disappear. They tend to fester and grow into even bigger problems.

Second, avoiding your feelings stops you from discovering how to manage them better. Think about it. If you run from a stressful situation what do you learn about it? What do you learn about yourself? Little! Personal growth occurs when you confront difficulties. If you stay, calm yourself down, and seek to handle things differently, then you learn from your coping actions and are likely to be more effective in the future.

Time-out strategies do have a place. Taking some time to cool down may be important if you risk harming others in your fury. Also, if you are learning how to manage your anger outbursts, taking a break may be useful in the early stages of change. As a long-term strategy, however, time-out will hinder your gaining emotional control and handling difficulties effectively. It just helps you avoid them.

MYTH NO. 3: ANGER PUSHES YOU TO GET WHAT YOU WANT

Perhaps, like many people, you believe that your anger helps you get what you want. Or that anger pushes you to overcome adversity and injustice. As we discussed in chapter 1, far from helping you to achieve your goals, it is more likely to get in your way.

Do you believe that without your temper outbursts, people will not listen to you, respect you, or comply with your wishes? Yes, some may not. And some people may bend to your rage. Your spouse or your children may do what you want to get you to call off your wrath. Your coworkers may also attempt to mollify your fury. So what's wrong with that?

Well, people *may* fulfill your desires while you are yelling or threatening—but mainly because of your constant pressure. Over time, they are likely to become resentful, bitter, or distant. This is what happened with Ned and his family:

> Ned was in his late forties when he came into treatment. He had been married for twenty-seven years and had two children, around whom he was very critical and demanding. Under Ned's barrage of criticism and hostility his wife, Nora, and his children would often comply with his wishes just to shut him up. Nora reported that the whole family was "walking on eggshells." They silently concluded that it was easier not to openly discuss almost anything with Ned. So everyone tiptoed around him.

While Ned often got his way in the short run, his family eventually learned ways to sabotage his control. The result: little trust and intimacy.

Many clients we have worked with make the mistake of looking only at the short-term rewards of their hostility. People may comply with your wishes. They may jump at your irate commands. Don't ignore the more damaging long-term costs of your "success," however. It will often destroy your relationship over the long haul.

MYTH NO. 4: INSIGHT INTO YOUR PAST DECREASES YOUR ANGER

This is another myth that is often instilled by mental health professionals. These "helpers" hold that in order to deal with your anger, you must get in touch with and replay the childhood traumas that once made and still keep you enraged. If you accept this myth, you can spend years in therapy trying to figure out why you are the way you are. Many therapists will happily explore with you every detail of your childhood and adolescent development. While this self-exploration can be interesting, will it help you decrease your anger? Hardly!

In order to test this idea, let's look at an analogy. Let's say you play tennis and would like very much to improve your game. So you go out and hire a tennis coach to help you. After several lessons and observations, the coach is able to identify or diagnose some of the reasons why you are not playing better. He points out that you hold the racket at a slightly wrong angle. Also, your stance when hitting the ball is awkward and incorrect.

How effective would the coach be if he spent months trying to help you figure out *how* you developed your awkward tennis style? Perhaps you learned your grip when playing tennis with your sister at summer camp? Or maybe you developed poor tennis posture in gym in the fifth grade? Would these insights help you play a better game of tennis? Rarely! For you to improve, it does not help to discover where or how you developed your awkward style.

It would be much more useful if you and your coach spent time learning and practicing a new hand grip and posture. Of course, these new skills won't feel quite right at first, because you are comfortable with your old habits. But with repetition and practice your new grip and stance will begin to feel right and help you to improve your game.

Naturally, learning to be less angry requires awareness of what you are doing wrong. But insight into how you developed your errors is not necessarily helpful. Learning and practicing new ways of thinking and behaving are more likely to help you play a better emotional tennis game.

You may, of course, have suffered early abuse, neglect, and mistreatment that helped you to become enraged. But focusing today on the horror of such past mistreatment hardly leads you to healthier functioning. Instead, your learning how to reframe those experiences and to challenge some of the anger-creating beliefs you still have about them will help you to reduce your present rage.

MYTH NO. 5: OUTSIDE EVENTS MAKE YOU ANGRY

When people get angry they often fail to take responsibility for their own feelings. How many times have you thought or said, "He made me angry," "She pissed me off," or "They made me furious"? With these types of statements you imply that your angry feelings lie outside of your control. You are, alas, just a helpless victim whose emotions have to dramatically rise and fall depending on how the world treats you.

If outside events really made us angry, we would all respond the same way to similar happenings. For example, take a situation where ten people are stuck in a traffic jam and are late for an important meeting. Will all ten respond exactly the same way? Of course not.

Some stuck people may make themselves visibly enraged, honking their horns, yelling at other drivers, and thinking, "Why do these creeps have to be driving so poorly? I could kill them!" Other drivers may seethe inside and say to themselves, "Why didn't I give myself more time? I should have started earlier. What an idiot I am!" Still others may remain calm, reminding themselves, "These kinds of things happen occasionally to most people. Too bad!"

Different people react differently to the same events. In fact, you rarely respond the same way at all times to the same situation. What accounts for these different emotional reactions? In most cases, your *beliefs* about the things that are happening determine your emotional responses. In the case of anger, when you are frustrated your reactions may feel almost automatic. Your rage may *seem* to just happen in response to outside events. As we shall keep showing in this book, however, you can fairly easily make yourself aware of the beliefs that lead you to create and keep yourself stuck in anger. You—and not those other rotten people—create your rage. Indeed, yes!

To successfully reduce your anger and more sanely face life's difficulties, give up the idea that unfair situations, difficult people, and great frustrations automatically *make* you furious. Yes, they help. But you still largely create what you feel. To accept that responsibility is a crucial first step in dealing effectively with your anger.

These five myths are some of the most common we have observed in our clients who have sought help for their anger problems. There are many other fallacies about anger, as Carol Tavris, Bud Nye, and other writers have emphasized. For now, though, accept, as a start, the five we have just described, and you can nicely proceed with our following chapters on how to live with and without angry feelings.

3

REBT and the ABC's of Anger

YOUR UNDERSTANDING AND USING the ABC's of REBT can give you a more satisfactory approach to the problem of dealing with your anger than you probably ever thought possible. It is not a magical formula, though. REBT seeks solutions to your problems and deals with them realistically, not magically.

How did REBT get started? What makes it different from other forms of psychotherapy?

I (AE) created the principles of REBT from my own clinical research and experience. Later, these principles were backed up by hundreds of experimental studies. During my career as a therapist I have used many different techniques in treating my clients. Years of intense clinical experience and research convinced me that most of the popular therapies—especially classical psychoanalysis, which I practiced for several years—are inefficient, and too expensive and time-consuming for both clients and therapists. So in 1953 I began looking for better procedures.

I drew many of the principles of REBT from the wisdom of philosophy as well as from psychology. Since my youth I have made the study of philosophy a main hobby; and by incorporating some of its principles into therapy, I discovered that my clients could achieve better results in far less time than when I used non-philosophic approaches. So in January 1955 I originated REBT and have helped train thousands of therapists in it since that time. Following my lead in the 1960s and 1970s, Aaron Beck, David

Burns, William Glasser, Maxie Maultsby Jr., Donald Meichen-baum, and other outstanding therapists started to do Cognitive Behavior Therapy (CBT), which closely resembles REBT in many respects. CBT is a general form of therapy that was patterned after REBT and uses many of REBT's theories and practices. However, it doesn't emphasize people's absolutistic shoulds and musts as much as REBT does and is less emotive and experiential than is REBT. This book will show you how to specifically use REBT but also how to apply CBT to your anger and other emotional problems.

Because the authors of this book are practicing therapists, we naturally advise you to see a competent REBT or CBT practitioner when you have a serious emotional problem. But we have found that by using REBT, you can also "therapize" yourself. In this book we will explain how you largely create your own anger *philosophically*—by resorting to absolutistic, command-oriented thinking. Therefore, if you understand how to observe and control your own thoughts, you will empower yourself to reduce your destructive anger.

REBT includes self-teaching methods to help you deal with your rage even under unusually trying circumstances. Even when you are unjustly abused and cheated? Yes, even then!

To show you how to healthily control your intense feelings of anger, rage, and vindictiveness, let us turn to an example. Imagine that Jack and Joan have promised to share an apartment with you as roommates and to share the rent, provided you fix up and furnish the place. This seems agreeable to you. You go to a good deal of trouble and personal expense to keep your part of the bargain. At the last minute they inform you that they have made other plans and cannot keep their part of the agreement. You feel extremely angry with them. Not only have you gone to considerable expense, but you must at the last minute look for someone else to share the apartment with you.

How can you effectively deal with your anger? You may at first keep your feelings to yourself. But because you still have them, your underlying resentment greatly interferes with your friendship with Joan and Jack. So you resolve nothing, and your rage interferes with your other activities. This solution won't work.

You may decide to confront Jack and Joan with your feelings, to *freely express* them. "Look here," you say, "I won't have you treating me like this! After all, you did say you'd share the apartment with me after I had fixed it up and furnished it. I never would have done that had you not agreed to share it with me in the first place. You've clearly done me wrong, and acted really rotten. How could you have done a thing like that to a friend? I've never done anything so nasty to you, and I really don't see how you can expect anyone's friendship if you treat people so terribly."

By openly voicing your anger, you may be rightly showing Joan and Jack how wrong they are. But you are still criticizing both their behavior (the deed) and them (the doers). By doing so you will often push them into being defensive and denying and encourage them to lash back angrily at you.

Don't forget that Jack and Joan, like most of the human race, probably have some strong self-blaming tendencies. Therefore, when you point out their errors they tend to feel worse than you intended them to feel. As a result of your critical remarks, no matter how well or creatively you put them, your friends may make themselves feel terribly guilty, and will frequently attempt to make you feel guilty, too. So honestly expressing your anger may harm both you and them.

Another alternative—that of *Christian forgiveness*—involves your turning the other cheek. But in our often exploitative and hostile world this can be impractical. People will feel less intimidated by you—but perhaps all the more tempted to take advantage of your passivity or good nature. You may indeed behave beautifully. But that hardly means that others will respect you and treat you as well as you treat them.

In viewing the above alternatives for dealing with anger, you can see that although each may *sometimes* work, applying it across the board has real drawbacks. So let us look for solutions that will allow you to deal with difficult situations and get what you want without being dishonest or encouraging return hostility and defensiveness in others or setting yourself up for further mistreatment.

We think we can safely say that no perfect method exists for dealing with disruptive anger. But let us present some procedures commonly used in REBT and in Cognitive Behavior Therapy (CBT) that have now been successful for more than four decades in helping people handle their rage. If you take the trouble to think seriously about and experiment with the REBT and CBT practices which we are about to describe, and if you practice them over a period of time, we believe that you, too, will learn to effectively handle your anger—as we have already helped so many of our clients to do.

How, by using REBT methods, can you deal with your hostility? Let us examine the ABC's of REBT.

We begin by locating C—the *emotional* (or *behavioral*) *Consequence:* your anger.

Next we look for A—the *Activating Experience* or *Adversity:* Joan and Jack failed to uphold their part of an important agreement with you.

As we look at A and C, it may appear that A causes C. REBT theory assumes, however, that although your Activating Experience directly contributes to your emotional Consequence, anger, it does not really *cause* it. For if you look closely at the relationship between A and C—as we will do throughout this book—you will indeed find that your friends' withdrawing from your agreement inconveniences and disappoints you greatly—because they are preventing you from getting what you wanted. But their withdrawal *alone* does not necessarily lead to your feeling angry with them. Hardly!

For if your anger, C, directly results from A, then we have to assume that whenever you encounter any one particular A, you always feel the same emotion at C. In fact, however, you don't. For instance, we know that water boils at one temperature and freezes at another and this is true for all situations involving water and temperature. Yet when people and situations interact, such physical laws do not hold true. We often feel surprised by a person's reaction to a given situation. For instance, we hear of crime victims who, instead of cooperating with the authorities to bring the criminal to justice, do the opposite. Oddly enough, they actually help their assailant avoid prosecution. If we examine one hundred people, all victims of the same crime, we will find many different responses. Some will act forgivingly, others will press for the harshest penalty available, and yet others will respond between these two extremes. An emotional Consequence, although affected by an Activating Experience, does not directly result from it.

Obviously, then, we have *some* degree of choice and control over our responses to various situations. The more aware we are of our possible responses to injustices, the more likely we are to consider reacting without rage. We are able to create Beliefs (B's) *between* A and C. Our B's about A largely determine our response to it. The more we make ourselves aware of our Beliefs *about* A, the better chance we have of making choices that help us achieve our goals. Through choosing to *think* about Adversities (A's), we stop acting too impulsively or foolishly at C. Unfortunately, we rarely reflect on our thinking; therefore, we seldom change the influence our thoughts have upon our actions and reactions.

You, like every other person, have developed a *Belief System* (B) that you rely upon to make judgments and evaluate people and events. Although you have your own personal Belief or value system, you also hold many Beliefs similar to others in your given family and culture. In some important ways, the Belief Systems of different cultures significantly differ and, over time, also change within a given culture. You as an individual may hold a number of different Belief Systems at once; you sometimes radically change your feelings and opinions in order to remain happy and productive in an ever-changing world.

Your individual Beliefs are not entirely your own. Much of what you view as good or bad, right or wrong, you have imbibed from your elders and from your social group.

Although your Belief System strongly influences your reactions at C, B is not the only factor in determining C. A also considerably influences your reactions. C, then, equals A times B. You often cannot effect any major influence over A, although you can determinedly try. Fortunately, you can usually change B—as we shall see.

None of your experiences has any set value in and of itself. You *give* them value. That is your nature—to value and to rate your experiences. What you desire and prefer you call "good" and what you dislike you call "bad." Once you rate or evaluate experiences (A's)—create Beliefs about them—your B's determine your feelings and behaviors that accompany these A's.

Knowing what your A's and C's are, you can easily figure out your B's and deal better with your C's, especially with your destructive self-blame and rages. Thus, starting with your rage (C) about, say, some unfairness you have experienced (A), you can quickly figure out your Irrational Beliefs (IBs) leading to C and can Dispute them (point D) by challenging their accuracy and usefulness. We shall show you how in the next chapter.

By starting with C (Consequences), you learn that your feeling of anger (or any other self-defeating feeling) follows a "negative" experience at A. You can also see that your Belief System strongly influences your feelings at C. At this point REBT helps you discover exactly what Beliefs contribute to your unhealthy negative feelings of anger and shows you how you can alter any of your Beliefs by examining their irrationality. It shows you how self-helping or Rational Beliefs (RBs) often make you healthily sorry and disappointed instead of enraged (C), how self-defeating or Irrational Beliefs (IBs) tend to make you angry (C) about Adversities (A's), and how you can Dispute (D) your IBs to make your feelings healthy and unenraged again.

4

Rational and Irrational Aspects of Anger

IN THIS CHAPTER we will attempt to show how your rational, helpful Beliefs and your irrational, unhelpful Beliefs fall into only a few major categories—and how you can learn to recognize and change your self-defeating Beliefs. Let us start, as we usually do, with C in the ABC's of REBT. At point C (Consequence), when something goes wrong in your life at point A, we look for two kinds of negative feelings. These tend to be:

Healthy negative feelings—such as disappointment, regret, and frustration
Unhealthy negative feelings—such as depression, panic, rage, self-pity, and low frustration tolerance.

Although no strict definition exists for either of these categories, we may say that healthy negative feelings and behaviors will help you cope with and overcome troubles and problems and achieve your major goals. These healthy negative feelings help you live happily and productively without unnecessary frustration and pain. On the other hand, unhealthy negative feelings tend to stop you from achieving many of your main goals.

We can also divide your Belief System (B) into two basic categories:

Constructive or Rational Beliefs (RBs)
Destructive or Irrational Beliefs (IBs).

We may safely assume that practically all humans have many Rational Beliefs. Otherwise, the human race could hardly survive. As noted before, we learn many of our Rational Beliefs, as well as our Irrational Beliefs, from our elders. But as George Kelly, Jean Piaget, and others have shown, we also construct many of them ourselves. Why do we do so? Because we are natural problem solvers and easily create both self-helping and self-sabotaging ideas.

When something unfortunate happens to you at A (Activating Experience or Adversity), and you feel disturbed at C (emotional Consequence), you have both RBs and IBs. If your RBs are stronger (more forceful) than your IBs, you usually do not feel disturbed (anxious or angry) at C; but if your IBs are stronger, you usually do feel disturbed at C.

Let us return to our illustration and see if we can locate your RBs. We know that you feel angry at Jack and Joan at C after they unfairly withdrew from an important agreement (A). You may therefore be saying to yourself (at B) something like: "What a bad thing they have done to me. How terrible that those worms are treating me so unfairly!" This may seem a rational or reasonable statement. Nonetheless, looking closer, we can see that although you appear to have only one idea here, you in fact have two contradictory ideas.

First, you are thinking, "What a bad thing they have done to me. They have seriously frustrated my plans, and not only greatly inconvenienced me, but also unfairly placed me in a very difficult situation." Your observation that Joan and Jack have done a bad thing to you seems both accurate and realistic.

Second, you are telling yourself, "How terrible that these worms are treating me so unfairly!" Here you see what Jack and Joan have done as "bad" *and* as "terrible," and you wind up with an Irrational Belief. Your belief that their action is terrible or horrible is irrational for several reasons: (1) By calling their act "terrible" you are implying that it is probably 100 percent bad or totally bad or as bad as it could be. These are exaggerations, because their act—let's face it—was not *that* bad. (2) You are strongly suggesting that their behavior is so bad that it *absolutely should not* exist and that Joan and

Jack have no right to make it exist. Actually, their unfair treatment of you *must* exist—because it indubitably *does* exist. And they *do* have the right—meaning the prerogative—to do right or wrong things. They have the *freedom* to behave as badly as they wish. (3) You are claiming that Jack and Joan did an unfair or lousy deed— and by normal cultural standards, you are correct. But you are also saying that they *are* worms and that their whole being and essence *is*, and presumably will always be, wormy. Quite an overgeneraliz- ation and an exaggeration! (4) Where will your "awfulizing" about what they did and your damning their whole personhood, for a fairly small part of their behavior—where will those Beliefs get you? Answer: In a hell rather similar to the one to which you are condemning them. You will thereby make yourself very enraged, may well do foolish things because of your fury, may easily encourage Jack and Joan to be furious at you, and may spark other kinds of needless unpleasantness for everybody.

Can you see why your reactions—and overreactions!—to your friends' unfair treatment of you can be more harmful than helpful? Give this some real thought!

By giving your IBs the power to overwhelm your RBs you tend to ignore reality, think illogically, court additional trouble, and impede your having healthy feelings and acting constructively. REBT shows you that unless you are aware of and work at changing your IBs, you will keep having difficulty in dealing with your anger and other disturbed feelings. It includes many emotive techniques of changing these feelings and many activity-oriented methods of improving your behavior. *But it holds that if you want to change your feelings and your actions most effectively, you'd better pay particular attention to changing your Belief System.*

Let us review: At A we know that Joan and Jack have treated you unfairly by withdrawing from your agreement.

- When considering our RBs, your Rational Belief System, we have discovered that you believe, "I don't like that. I wish they hadn't treated me so shabbily."
- At C, your healthy emotional Consequence, you experience

feelings of disappointment, displeasure, and discomfort.

* *Rational Belief:* "I don't like what's going on." Healthy negative feelings: disappointment, frustration, regret.

By contrast, if we find that at C, you are enraged at Jack and Joan (your unhealthy Consequence), you will want to use REBT to seek the IBs that led to this C (anger).

To discover and uproot your IBs, you use the REBT method of Disputing (D), designed to discover any unrealistic and illogical Beliefs that you hold at B. By putting your anger into an REBT framework, you can discover your RBs and IBs through first observing what is happening at A and C. For example, one of your RBs is, "How obnoxious of Jack and Joan to make an agreement with me and then suddenly withdraw." This Belief *does* make sense, as just about everyone would agree. Also, your merely viewing their behavior as obnoxious will likely lead you to feel healthy disappointment instead of destructive rage.

So you keep observing your Beliefs, to discover what else you have thought. You then see that you also told yourself, "It is *awful* that Joan and Jack behaved so irresponsibly! This is most unfair and *terrible!*" Although this Belief may not at first glance seem very irrational or illogical, it is, in fact, one of the four irrational statements that people often make to create—yes, create—their rage. For when you say that it is *awful*, *horrible*, or *terrible* that Jack and Joan have treated you badly, you have equated their *unfairness* with *horror* and failed to see that the two are different.

What are the four main IBs that you—and billions of other people—invent to make themselves angry, furious, enraged, and sometimes homicidal? Usually, these:

1. "How *awful* for people to treat me so inconsiderately and unfairly!"
2. "I *can't stand* their treating me that way!"
3. "They *absolutely should not*, *must not* behave so badly!"
4. "Because they are acting so wickedly, they are *terrible people* who don't deserve a good life, and who should be punished!"

These self-upsetting statements are all related and tend to blame people's "bad" behaviors on their entire person. This merging of a person with his action implies that only a "good" person can act "well" and that all "bad" acts must be performed by "rotten" people. To make things more confusing, any person who does anything that any other person deems "bad" must *be* a "bad person." If a "good person" acts, then she presumably can *never* do anything bad, for she *is* a "good person" and capable of only "good" acts. Again, if a "bad person" acts, he can *never* do anything "good," for he *is* a bad person and can only perform "bad" deeds.

Actually, we know that people who are seen as good and responsible often unjustly treat others. Also, people who have acted very fairly in a number of situations are sometimes labeled as "bad people" by many others. So we'd better watch this kind of overgeneralizing!

Back to the problem of your angering yourself at Joan and Jack and your viewing them as rotten when they do a rotten act. Using REBT, you can see that your unhealthy Consequence, rage, stems from your correctly connecting them and their irresponsible actions and *also* from your incorrectly damning them—their entire persons for these actions. To remain rational—that is self-helping and social-helping—you can evaluate Joan and Jack's unjust behavior while refusing to put them down as "horrible people."

Because you have judged Joan and Jack's conduct—and not their whole personhood—as obnoxious, and because their withdrawing from your agreement has seriously inconvenienced you, you may now wisely decide not to enter into any further agreement with them. By giving up your rage, you leave open the possibility of reestablishing good relations with them, for you still can acknowledge some of their good qualities. And because you do not totally reject them, you help them observe your good judgment, respect you as a person, and perhaps encourage them to act more fairly to you in the future.

As you can see from this example, REBT principles not only deal with the destructive aspects of anger but also often provide the groundwork for reestablishing relationships on the basis of mutual respect. As pointed out earlier, one of the first casualties of your anger may well be the loss of close relationships.

We have thus far explained the basic principles of the REBT theory. The next chapter will examine various methods you can use to help detect IBs with which you largely create destructive anger.

5

Discovering Your Rage-Creating Beliefs

INSIGHT INTO YOUR PAST AND PRESENT is fascinating. But not enough! Knowing how you first made yourself angry and are continuing to do so today is highly important. So REBT shows you what you originally did to get your anger started and what you are now doing to keep it going.

In this chapter we shall look into what you formerly did, are still doing, and will tend to keep doing to create destructive rage. More important, we shall show how you can use this insight to change your anger-creating ways.

Is REBT insight into your anger similar to psychoanalytic insight? Heck, no!—it is deeper and more useful. If you present your problem of rage to an analyst, he will probably spend the next several years showing you how your family treated you badly in your early years and thereby made you furious, and how you are transferring your early rage to your present intimates and thus neurotically upsetting yourself today.

Even if this insight is correct, will it really help you? Most unlikely! At best, it informs you about the *conditions* that created and that now sustain your anger, but it doesn't reveal your early and present Beliefs *about* these conditions or teach you how to *change* these Beliefs.

REBT insight reveals your *philosophy* about your family's presumable early mistreatment and your *attitudes* about your present victimization. It shows you that however you were influenced during your suggestible childhood, you are *still* reinfluencing yourself today. And it shows you that as a thinking person, you can now *radically change* your anger-inciting Beliefs today. Yes, change.

Going beyond psychoanalysis, REBT stresses that as an adult, you now have conscious *choices*. You—not your family or others—can now make and direct these choices. As an adult, you *can* control your ideas, attitudes, and actions. You largely *can* arrange your life according to your own dictates—if you *work* at doing so.

Many of our clients, when they become aware of their IBs, tell us they got them from their parents. Yes, but they still choose to *maintain* these irrationalities. Moreover, as REBT stresses, both children and adults are *creative*. They take their desires and preferences, which they partly learn from their parents and culture, and they often turn them into self-defeating demands and commands—absolutistic shoulds, oughts, and musts. So they learn to be, but they *also* creatively make themselves into, self-defeating *mus*turbators. Yes, the beliefs that people hold partly stem from ideas they acquired as children and never gave up in their adult lives. But they also originate in their *own* creative talent for inventing crooked ways of thinking.

Let us now return to our REBT model and show you how to use the insights you are acquiring to discover and minimize your goal-inhibiting IBs. In the last chapter we showed that disturbed reactions (C's) to Adversities (A's) largely involve IBs. At this point we ask: What does B consist of? More important, what RBs and IBs do you hold?

You can use two approaches to locate your RBs and your IBs. First you ask, "What do I seem to believe at B just before I experience my disturbed Consequences at C?" If you don't get a clear answer, you can then try the second approach. You know both A and C. If C is unhealthy—such as anger, anxiety, or depression—you may well assume that some kind of IB influenced your feeling. We have already listed the four IBs with which most people create their anger. But once again:

1. "How *awful* or *terrible* that you treat me like this!"
2. "I *can't stand* your irresponsible behavior!"
3. "You *should not* and *must not* act in that bad manner toward me!"
4. "Because you behave as you should not and must not, you are a *rotten person* and should be *severely punished!*"

Although these statements hold for anger, they often apply a little differently when you experience anxiety, rather than anger, at C. You make yourself anxious when you are afraid that you will not get something you really want—such as success or pleasure—and when you demand or command that you *absolutely must* get it. Anxiety usually stems from IBs that you hold about yourself, while anger stems from IBs that you hold about others.

Using our illustration, let us say that you have received an indirect signal or message from Jack and Joan that they will withdraw from your agreement with them. Suppose you hear that they hinted to a friend about breaking their agreement with you. You do not yet know for certain that they will withdraw and hesitate to confront them about this issue. So at point A you think they may withdraw but are in doubt about this. At point C you make yourself feel anxious. What are your IBs that largely create your anxiety (C)? They probably are:

1. "How *awful* if Joan and Jack withdraw from our agreement! I won't be able to manage the apartment and that would be *terrible*!"
2. "I couldn't, under such conditions, *bear* the inconvenience they would be foisting on me!"
3. "I *shouldn't have* let them get me into this fix and I'm a *weakling* for allowing this!"
4. "If I don't cope as well as I *must* cope with their possible withdrawal, I am an *inferior person*, and I deserve what I get for not handling the situation as I *should* be able to handle it!"

As you can easily see, the above IBs that make you anxious are similar to those that make you angry. The main difference is that you hold these Beliefs about yourself rather than about Jack and Joan.

Another way you may create unhealthy negative feelings at point C and thereby upset yourself unnecessarily might be as follows. Let us say that instead of withdrawing from the agreement with you, Joan and Jack got transferred to another location and had to move out of town. You realize that they had relatively little choice in this matter because they could only keep their jobs by moving. So you understand their decision. But although you are not angry with Joan and Jack, you discover that you feel extremely depressed at point C. You then may have IBs like these:

1. "How *awful* that things have turned out so badly for me!"
2. "I *can't stand* things turning out this way!"
3. "Things *shouldn't* happen this way, and be so terribly inconvenient!"
4. "Nothing ever works out the way I want it to. Life is *always unfair* to me—as it *shouldn't* be!"

Obviously the above Beliefs are irrational and self-defeating. Yet just about all of us have such ideas when we depress ourselves. This tends to show that the kinds of IBs that produce anger, anxiety, and depression are fairly similar. Anger-producing IBs put *others* down. Anxiety-inciting IBs put *yourself* down. And depression-creating IBs sometimes put *world conditions* down.

REBT practitioners keep encountering numerous IBs that people hold and use to make themselves angry, anxious, and depressed. Yet upon examination we have found that we can place just about all these IBs under three major *must*urbatory headings: (1) *Anxiety and depression:* "I *absolutely must* do well and be approved of by significant others!" (2) *Anger and rage:* "You *must* treat me kindly and fairly!" (3) *Low frustration tolerance, anger,* and *depression:* "Conditions *must* be the way I want them to be!" These dogmatic musts seem to be basic to practically all human neurosis. Then, when they are not actually fulfilled—as of course is often the case—people who musturbate tend to make several "logical" conclusions:

1. *Awfulizing*—"It is *awful* that I'm doing so badly (when I *absolutely should* do better)!" "It's terrible when you treat me unkindly (when you *absolutely must* treat me more considerately)!"

2. *Can't-stand-it-itis*—"When you treat me poorly (as you *absolutely must not*) I can't stand it!" "When conditions are really bad for me (as *they absolutely must not* be), I can't tolerate them!"

3. *Damnation*—"When I act very badly (as I *absolutely must not*) I am a rotten damnable person who deserves to suffer!" "When I act very stupidly and incompetently (as I *absolutely should not*) I am a worthless, thoroughly inadequate person!" "When you treat me shabbily and unfairly (as you *absolutely should* never do) you are a damnable, completely rotten person!"

4. *All or nothingism; overgeneralization*—"If I fail a few times at an important goal (which I *absolutely must not*) I'll *always* fail, *never* succeed, and will prove that I am no good!" "If you treat me very unkindly and unjustly (as you *absolutely must* not), you *are* a rotten person who will *never* treat me well!"

You will note that when you—like other people—make yourself disturbed, you tend to use one or more of these IBs. Sometimes all of them! You *awfulize* about unfortunate Adversities (A's). You insist that you *can't stand* them. You damn yourself, other people, and world conditions for producing them. You overgeneralize about them and see them in all-or-nothing, black-and-white terms. You not only give *importance* and *significance* to unfortunate Activating Events or Adversities, you also *greatly exaggerate* them—take them *too* seriously.

Why? Because that's what humans often tend to do. Not *have* to do, but *tend* to do. To stay alive and make themselves happy, they usually have to prioritize or emphasize several things—such as getting enough air, food, water, and shelter. Otherwise, they would die. And they *preferably* should prioritize many other things—such as getting along with other people, having some intimate relationships, working at a suitable job or profession, having long-range goals and purposes, and enjoying some recreational pursuits. Otherwise, they will survive rather miserably.

So REBT says that your *shoulds* are okay as long as they are *preferably* shoulds. Thus, you can sensibly believe, "I *preferably* should succeed, win people's approval, and be comfortable—but I don't *have to*. I *can* live and be reasonably happy even if I fail, gain disapproval, and live with discomfort." You can also believe, "If I want certain results—such as getting and holding a good job—then I have to apply for it, have a favorable interview, come regularly to work, get along with my supervisors, etc. But it's not *absolutely necessary* that I get and hold a good job. Only very *desirable!*"

REBT particularly stresses the poor results you will usually—though not always—get from imperative *shoulding* and *musting*. As noted above, you disturb and handicap yourself with three basic or core demands: "I *absolutely must* perform well!" "Other people *must always* act nicely!" and "Conditions *always have to be* the way I want them to be!" To make yourself feel needlessly angry, anxious, or depressed, you almost always escalate your desires into assumed needs, your preferences into demands and insistences, your relative wishes into absolute dictates.

Whenever you feel truly disturbed emotionally, you tend to resort to one, two, or all three of these forms of musturbation. Many human problems have little or nothing to do with inner demands, but emotional problems usually stem from these forms of thinking and behaving. After talking with thousands of people with varying degrees of upset, we still haven't found any who do not themselves, with their own self-verbalizing hatchets, create much of their unnecessary emotional disturbances.

Practically all men and women have scores of important IBs, any one of which can contribute to their difficulties. As already noted, all these IBs seem to fit under only a few major headings. We shall now describe some common variations of these Irrational Beliefs that contribute to or cause emotional disturbances.

IRRATIONAL ACHIEVEMENT AND APPROVAL MUSTS

"I must do well, win the approval of others, and never get rejected or else I am a rotten, inadequate person."

Once you believe this idea, as many people in all parts of the world often seem to do, you may then somewhat logically conclude: "If I am a rotten or inferior person, I will rarely or never succeed at important projects, so what's the use of trying to do so?"

This irrational achievement and approval must is self-defeating because it often leads to strong feelings of anxiety, depression, worthlessness, and self-hatred and to avoidance, procrastination, inhibition, and other withdrawing behaviors.

To make matters worse, when you demand that you *must* perform well and *must* be accepted by others, you actually act less adequately and bring on the emotional and behavioral problems just mentioned. You then frequently musturbate about these symptoms: "I must not feel anxious! I must avoid projects at which I might fail!" You have then created secondary symptoms *about* your primary symptoms—especially anxiety about your anxiety and depression about your depression—and now make yourself *doubly* upset!

IRRATIONAL MUSTS ABOUT OTHERS

"Others *absolutely* must treat me considerately and kindly and in precisely the way I want them to treat me. If they don't, they are bad people and should be damned and punished for their awful behavior."

This irrational must often makes you angry, nasty, mean, combative and/or vindictive—and, of course, often encourages the people you dislike to treat you worse than ever. Also, you may easily tell yourself, "I *must not* be angry and vindictive!" and can thereby make yourself angry at *you* for being angry at *them*.

IRRATIONAL MUSTS ABOUT LIFE CONDITIONS

"The world (and the people in it) *must* be arranged so that I get practically everything that I really want when I want it. And further, conditions *must* be arranged so that I don't get what I don't want. Moreover, I usually must get what I want quickly and easily."

These self-defeating demands create your low frustration tolerance or discomfort disturbance. When you strongly think this way you feel angry at bad conditions and often rebel against changing or coping with them. You tend to feel depressed and hopeless, to give up and withdraw, and to whine and scream that things are *awful* and that you *can't stand* them. Then you may put yourself down for having such low frustration tolerance.

These three core IBs have, of course, scores of variations. But we can note again that when you hold them they encourage you to resort to awfulizing, to I-can't-stand-it-itis, to damning yourself and others, and to ineffective overgeneralizing.

6

Special Insights Into Your Self-Angering Beliefs

WE START AGAIN WITH ONE of the basic principles of REBT: Other people may really try to get you angry but, as Eleanor Roosevelt said about making you feel inferior, they need your permission to do so. You—y-o-u—normally anger yourself. You do so by creating IBs *about* others' "unfair" and "unjust" behaviors. Let us now show you how to achieve three important REBT insights into your anger-creating Beliefs.

Insight No. 1 is that, yes, your present anger may have *some* connection with your past life—but not as much as Freudian and other psychologists often try to convince you. When you feel angry today (at point C) the Adversities (A's) that you are enraged about *contribute* to C but do not directly *cause* it. Instead, your current Beliefs (B's) *about* "unjust" A's largely and more directly "cause" C. Yes, your early traumas may have been important to this process, but they are hardly crucial. Your *present* Adversities and your *current* Beliefs about them are even *more* important. You will find this position, of course, distinctly contrary to that held by several other methods of therapy.

We do not say that your past experiences have *no* effect on your present behavior. For instance, researchers have found that children who are severely punished by their parents will develop a tendency to feel more anger and act more violently toward others throughout their lives than will children who are less violently or severely treated. While this indicates that to some degree, there is a relationship between a person's early training and his or her later conduct, we had better not view this information as conclusive.

We had better also consider possible genetic factors along with early environmental influences. The increased anger and violence of those raised in hostile circumstances may involve an inherited as well as an acquired disposition. For if parents have an inherited aggressive tendency, they may well pass it on to their child. If so, the parents may then react to the child's aggression with harsh discipline, which may in turn reinforce the child's violent disposition. This creates a vicious cycle of violence leading to more violence—a cycle that REBT seeks to break.

Insight No. 1 stresses the importance of the beliefs you hold today. In REBT, we don't dwell on how you arrived at those beliefs. The teachings you received from your parents and elders during your childhood may indeed have a great deal of influence upon your present Beliefs. Yet, as stated before, you can change these Beliefs, no matter how you may have acquired them. So it is interesting to discover *how* you came by your current IBs; but knowing what they are right *now* and working to change them— these are more important issues.

Now let us examine REBT **Insight No. 2:** However you may have originally acquired your self-defeating IBs, you now keep them alive by *repeating* them to yourself, *reinforcing* them in various ways, *acting* on them, and *refusing* to challenge them. Other people may have originally helped you acquire your IBs and even drilled many of them into you. But the primary reason you still subscribe to them is because you *still* brainwash yourself with them.

Insight No. 2 involves two closely related major points. First, you carry on your early anger-creating IBs by repeating them to yourself and often acting upon them. You seem to do this automatically or unconsciously, but if you look more closely you will see that you *actively* keep restating your IBs. Again, although it seems or feels as if your anger naturally persists once you make yourself hate someone, you actively *keep it alive* by frequently telling yourself that the person *absolutely should not* have behaved badly and is rotten for acting that way.

Second, REBT holds that your original frustration leading to rage has little to do with your holding and retaining your anger for prolonged periods of time. Your ongoing, or sustained, view of that original frustration—rather than the frustrating condition itself—keeps you persistently angry.

Suppose that you are very incensed because your parents abused you when you were a child. If you still hate them today, you most probably repeat the same Beliefs you told yourself years ago: "They unfairly and cruelly abused me when I was a child and they *absolutely should not, must not* have done so! What rotten people they are!"

Unless you repeat your IBs about your original Adversity, and thus force yourself to hold on to them, you would most probably not retain your rage at your parents although you still, of course, would remember and dislike what they did to you. So your ongoing, or sustained, *view* of your original Adversity, rather than it in its own right, would be the main thing that *keeps* you incensed.

Insight No. 3 of REBT states that in order to change your disturbed feelings and behaviors and the IBs that create them, you almost always have to do a great deal of work and practice. For no matter how aware you are of the self-defeating nature of your irrational attitudes and actions, your awareness does not help you unless you effectively Dispute and act against these ideas. And you can rarely do this without much practice and work.

All your beliefs, whether rational or irrational, range from weak to strong. For instance, you may hold certain superstitious beliefs, but to different degrees. Although you may rationally know that black cats and broken mirrors do not lead to bad luck, you may still avoid them because you believe that they do. This shows that there is a considerable difference between *telling* yourself that something is rational and really *convincing* yourself that it is.

Because Beliefs tend to vary in intensity, you'd better *strongly* Dispute your IBs at point D (Disputing). No matter how aware you are that a Belief is irrational, your insight will help you little unless you develop real skill in Disputing this IB. And unless you Dispute your IBs *powerfully*, you will still tend to follow them. Insight and knowledge *alone* often have little value.

Remember, the more powerfully and consistently you Dispute your anxiety-creating or anger-producing IBs, the sooner you will change them. The next chapter will outline basic strategies for examining and challenging your IBs.

7

Disputing Your Self-Angering Beliefs

In REBT, D represents Disputing. First, you find the Activating Experiences or Adversities (A's) that precede your disturbed Emotional or Behavioral Consequences (C's). Second, you discover your Rational Beliefs (RBs) and Irrational Beliefs (IBs) about your A's. Third, you clearly acknowledge that your IBs help create your disturbed or unhealthy Consequences (C's). Fourth, you vigorously and persistently Dispute your IBs.

Kishor Phadke, a psychologist who practices and teaches REBT in Bombay, breaks down Disputing (D) into three main parts:

Detection
Discriminating
Debating

Correct! Disputing does largely consist of detecting your main IBs, discriminating them clearly from your RBs, and then debating these IBs actively and vigorously. So far we have outlined the ABC's of anger and shown how you can detect your IBs that largely create it. We now will show how you can persistently and strongly discriminate your IBs from your RBs and then debate your IBs.

To begin this debating process, consider again the four major kinds of Irrational Beliefs that you tend to hold when you make yourself angry at people, and notice that each of them goes along with and can be discriminated from your Rational Beliefs that lead to *non*angry, healthy negative feelings when someone offends you:

1. *Rational Belief*: "I hate your treating me with verbal abuse and I strongly prefer that you stop it!" *Irrational Belief*: "You absolutely *must not* treat me with this verbal abuse. You *never should* act in that bad way toward me!"

2. *Rational Belief*: "Because you are treating me unfairly with your verbal abuse, your behavior is wrong and poor, and you preferably should correct it." *Irrational Belief*: "Because you are treating me unfairly with your verbal abuse, you *absolutely must not*; you are a rotten person who should be dammed and severely punished!"

3. *Rational Belief*: "It is highly unpleasant when you verbally abuse me, and I prefer you to stop it and feel bad about it." *Irrational Belief*: "It is *awful* and terrible when you verbally abuse me, as you *must* not! Nothing could be worse than this!"

4. *Rational Belief*: "I find it so unpleasant when you irresponsibly abuse me verbally that I want to stay away from you as much as I can." *Irrational Belief*: "I find it so unpleasant when you irresponsibly abuse me verbally, as you *must* not, that I *can't stand it*, can only feel anguish, and am unable to enjoy myself at all in any way!"

Each of the above statements starts with a rational *preference* and ends up with an irrational *command* that you must not be verbally abused. So, first, clearly see the difference between these two kinds of Beliefs. Then go on to maintain and uphold your RBs while strongly disputing your IBs. You can do this as follows:

Using our apartment-sharing illustration again, you may be telling yourself the Irrational Belief about Jack and Joan's treating you unfairly. "How awful that they made me go to so much trouble and then withdrew from our agreement."

Assuming that you devoutly believe this IB and that you want to challenge it, you first ask yourself, "Why is it *awful* for them to withdraw from our agreement without any good reason?" Or, in briefer form, "What makes their unfairness *awful*?"

You could, of course, show that Joan and Jack's behavior makes you suffer needless inconvenience and expense. True. But if you viewed it as only annoying and disadvantageous, you would feel disappointed and sorry—but not really angry. It's your *awfulizing* about their unfair behavior that sets off your unhealthy feeling of rage.

Your calling Jack and Joan's copping out on their agreement with you "bad" or "unjust" is okay, because you did have an agreement, they failed to follow it, and your goals and interests were thereby sabotaged. But your claiming that their behavior is *awful* and *terrible* implies several highly questionable extra Beliefs:

1. "Jack and Joan are treating me as badly as anyone could treat me. Nothing could be worse than their treatment of me!"
2. "They are really treating me 100 percent badly; therefore I can't enjoy this life *at all*!"
3. "They *absolutely should not*, *must not* treat me that badly."
4. "Being my friends, they *must absolutely not* treat me badly at all but *should* only treat me well, as friends especially *must* do!"

You can Dispute these dubious Beliefs by asking yourself the following questions and coming up with suitable answers as follows:

Disputing: "Did Jack and Joan treat me as badly as anyone could? Could nothing be worse than the way they dealt with me?"

Answer: "No, they treated me quite badly, but it could have been worse. They could have, for example, killed me! Or they could have moved in with me and continued to plague me in many ways."

Disputing: "Did they really treat me 100 percent badly? Can I therefore not enjoy life *at* all?"

Answer: "No. *Very* badly but hardly 100 percent. And no matter how badly they treated me, if I stop upsetting myself about their bad treatment, I *can* still enjoy life—though not as much as I would if they had treated me fairly."

Disputing: "Is there any reason why they *absolutely should* not, *must* not treat me as badly as they treated me?"

Answer: "Of course not. There are many reasons why it is

undesirable for them to treat me this way. But they *should* act undesirably when they do. That is obviously part of their nature to do so. They *have* to act badly when they act badly. Whatever *is* must, right now, *be*. And that's the rotten way it *is*!"

Disputing: "Is it true that, being my friends, they *must absolutely not* treat me badly *at all*, as friends especially *must not?*"

Answer: "Nonsense! Friends can treat me as badly as anyone else—and sometimes clearly do. Obviously, these particular "friends" are not that friendly. Well, they don't *have* to be! Next time, maybe I'd better make my apartment-sharing contracts with nonfriends!"

If you keep strongly and persistently Disputing your awfulizing and your musturbation about people's treating you—or your *thinking* that they have been treating you—unkindly and unfairly, you will still have distinct negative feelings. For REBT doesn't attempt to make you "rational" in the sense of ridding you of all your feelings. Not at all! It encourages you to have a number of negative feelings when things go wrong—or when you make them go wrong—such as sorrow, regret, disappointment, frustration, annoyance, and irritation. These, again, are *healthy* negative feelings, because they help you cope with Adversities, possibly overcome them, and, if necessary, gracefully accept and put up with them. So don't try to stop or stuff all your feelings!

Instead, distinguish your *unhealthy* negative feelings—such as rage, panic, depression, and self-pity—from your *healthy* negative emotions; and only look for, find, and Dispute the musturbation and awfulizing that lie behind the unhealthy feelings. Once you learn how to Dispute and change your absolutistic shoulds and musts and the awfulizing that usually accompanies them, you can carry on these skills for the rest of your life.

THE REBT SELF-HELP FORM

REBT, as we keep stressing throughout this book, teaches people many thinking, feeling, and behavioral methods of getting in touch with and reducing their destructive anger (and other self-defeating emotions), and it strongly encourages them to do steady homework assignments to practice these methods.

The main thinking homework that you can do to minimize your rage reactions consists of regularly filling out the REBT Self-Help Form in the Appendix, which is adapted from one originated in England by Windy Dryden and Jane Walker.

To show you how you can fill out a typical REBT Self-Help Form for one of your anger problems, we have included a sample completed form in the appendix as well.

8

More Ways of Thinking Yourself Out of Your Anger

ANTIAWFULIZING AND ANTIMUSTURBATION are basic to uprooting your feelings of anger, rage, resentment, and fury. You awfulize and resort to musturbation in several major ways; and once you tell yourself that something is *awful* and that it *must* not exist the way it does, you also frequently convince yourself of other related IBs. Let us now look at some of your other irrationalities and at what you can do to minimize them.

As already mentioned, REBT calls one of these beliefs *I-can't-stand-it-itis*. We frequently find this type of awfulizing in statements like: "Because you *must not* treat me unfairly, and you actually do so, I can't stand *it when you treat me that way!*"

What we call the Debating part of Disputing in REBT means asking yourself questions that will challenge your IBs. The main challenges consist of "Why?" "How?" "In what manner?" "What evidence exists for this?" "Where can I find the proof?" Thus, you ask yourself, "Why or in what manner can't I stand this unfair treatment?"

When you are enraged at Joan and Jack for backing out of their apartment-sharing deal with you, you may well tell yourself, "Because they have treated me exceptionally unfairly and have caused me great amounts of unnecessary harm, I *can't stand* their doing that to me."

You can now ask the question: "*Why* can't I stand it?" You probably see the situation as intolerable because you think you have experienced *too much* pain, *too much* suffering from Jack and Joan's unfair action. So you have escalated *much* pain and trouble into *too much* pain and trouble. The term "too," as used here, seems to take on a more or less magical quality. You presume that you can only allow Jack and Joan to give you *much* difficulty and inconvenience and *no more*. Therefore, you define the trouble they gave you as *too* much. Why is it too much? Because you say it is and not for any more precise or factual reason. Most people would agree with you that Joan and Jack caused you *much* frustration. But *too* much? Who is to say? Answer: Only you.

Indeed, whenever you believe that some frustration is *too* much and that therefore you can't stand it, you suffer not only from that frustration but from low frustration tolerance (LFT) as well. LFT is the tendency to rant and rave at, rather than merely dislike, frustration. Such ranting and raving makes you feel much more frustrated than you would otherwise.

If you Debate, and keep debating, your I-Can't-Stand-It-Itis, you will arrive at a more practical attitude for dealing with frustration. Anything that you believe you can also definitely *refuse* to believe. You cannot control to any great degree what actually exists, but you do control—almost completely—what you *think about* what exists. So while you have very little control over how Jack and Joan treat you (fairly or unfairly, well or badly), you do have much choice over the way in which you view their unfairness. Thus, even if you judge their actions as very unfair and if others agree that you have really been treated quite badly, you still can choose to believe this Effective New Philosophy (E):

1. "I *can* stand this unfairness, though I'll never like it."
2. "It is quite bad, but it is *not awful* and *terrible*."
3. "It is highly *preferable* that Jack and Joan treat me fairly, but they obviously don't *have* to do so."
4. "They are not *rotten* people but people who sometimes treat me rottenly."

Let us now Debate another IB: "Because Jack and Joan treated me unfairly, as they *absolutely should never have done*, they are *horrible, damnable people* who deserve nothing good in life!" How can you Dispute this IB and thereby continue to hate Jack and Joan's *behavior* without thoroughly and everlastingly hating *them?* How indeed?

First of all, rid yourself, once again, of your silly Belief that Joan and Jack *absolutely must* act nicely and morally. Because they are behaving against the usual rules of our culture, you can legitimately conclude that their acts are "wrong," "unfair," or "immoral." You can therefore also conclude, "It *would be better* if they acted rightly, fairly, and morally, but they obviously don't *have* to do so." As we explained in the previous chapter, first actively Debate your grandiose *musts* that you are carelessly foisting on Joan and Jack.

Once you surrender your musturbation about your two "friends" and their unfair treatment of you, you can fairly easily tackle your damning them as *persons* for acting so badly. Whenever you feel rage about people's actions, you have a human tendency to equate their *deeds* with their *selves* and to give them negative *global* ratings. We mentioned this before, but because antidamning of people is so important to emotional health, let us go into it in more detail here.

Actually, as Alfred Korzybski brilliantly showed in 1933 in *Science and Sanity*, there are no good and no bad people. For a "good person" would only and always do good deeds and never do bad ones. But even the saints did some bad deeds! And a "bad person" could only do vile acts. But even Hitler and Stalin did a few good deeds! *General* or *global* evaluations of anyone are misleading overgeneralizations and portray humans in all-white or all-black terms—which is certainly inaccurate!

Even though Jack and Joan, then, may have truly treated you extremely badly, you cannot accurately label them as extremely bad *people*. They surely have some good aspects. Ironically enough, when your hatred makes you damn them for their unfair behavior you are yourself acting unfairly to them! They are not lice, vermin, or devils. They are not subhuman. Realistically, they are fallible, somewhat screwed-up humans. As which of us—including yourself, of course—isn't?

Just as important: If you globally rate Joan and Jack as *rotten, evil, or worthless people*, how are you going to evaluate *yourself* when you act stupidly, badly, or unfairly? Pretty low, we'd say. For if you damn others for their errors, how can you not also damn yourself—your entire being or personhood—for *your* failings? Give some thought to that dilemma!

Your hating others as *persons*, in other words, borders much too close on *self*-hatred. By all means acknowledge your errors, faults, and wrongdoings. But if you put *yourself* down for committing them, how is a *no-goodnik* like you going to be able to correct your errors? How can a rotten person act nonrottenly in the future? Not very easily!

The same with Jack and Joan. If they really are worthless and damnable for treating you badly, how could they—or any other "criminal"—ever change and correct their ways? How indeed! So by putting them down for their deficiencies, you make them unforgivable—presumably doomed to do only bad deeds forever. Again, is that a fair global judgment of them?

That is why REBT opposes the concepts of both self-esteem and self-damnation, as well as deifying and damning other people. Self-esteem, as it is commonly understood today, implies and really seems to include self-condemnation. For if you esteem and like yourself for doing right, good, or fine things, you will most probably dislike and hate yourself when you do—as you *will* do!— wrong, bad, and improper things.

The same with other people. If you esteem them when they act well, you will tend to hate them when they behave badly. That won't get you very far—and it will tend to make you angry, furious, and vindictive. Then where are your friendly, cooperative, and helpful relationships with others? Not on too good a track!

Can you legitimately and usefully feel angry at some of the things that Jack, Joan, and other people *do* but still not feel angry at *them* for their doings? Yes. You can feel what we call "rational anger" when you are very annoyed and displeased only at people's thoughts, feelings, and actions and not at the people *themselves* for having these behaviors. Watch it, however! For almost all the time you do feel anger or rage at what people do, you somehow sneak in the demand that *they* absolutely should not act that way and that consequently *they*, as well as their deeds, are no damned good. But if you want to say—and really mean—"I am very angry at what Jack and Joan *did* to me but I still accept *them* as fallible, screwed-up humans who did the wrong *thing*," that's okay. *If* you really mean it!

REBT holds that you often go out of your way to (inaccurately) rate yourself not really to show that you are human, but to prove you are superhuman, or superior to virtually all other humans. When you strive for "self-esteem," you really strive for perfection, godlikeness, utter superiority, and nobility. You don't merely mean that some of your *traits* are better than or superior to those of others. You actually mean that you, your essence, is better than other people's essences. And you may also mean that if you don't excel more than other humans and become universally admired, you will have little or no real value.

Oddly enough, when you do something poorly, you see yourself as pretty worthless. But you may easily accept others with exactly the same deficiency. For example, if you write a poor essay, you may view yourself as a total failure who can never write well. Yet if someone writes equally poorly, you may readily accept his or her deficiency.

We do not question your evaluating and judging specific traits and characteristics in yourself and others. You may passionately like or dislike anything you choose. But don't carry your judgment of a trait into *other* areas of a person's total makeup.

Let us once again review the REBT theory regarding Joan and Jack's unfairly treating you in an apartment-sharing agreement.

Activating Experience or Adversity (A): Jack and Joan treat you unfairly by withdrawing from an agreement you have made.

Rational Belief (RB): "I find their action deplorable and unfortunate. I don't like it."

Healthy Negative Consequence (C): You feel frustrated and disappointed.

Irrational Belief (IB): "How awful! They *absolutely should not, must not* treat me this way!"

Unhealthy Negative Consequence (C): You feel angry and enraged.

Disputing and Debating (D): You detect your IBs and begin Disputing and Debating them by asking yourself questions about them: "Why is it *awful* that they are unfair? Where is it written that they *absolutely must not* be?"

Cognitive Effect or New Philosophy (E): "I can see no reason why they *must* treat me fairly even though I would definitely *prefer* it. It's painful when they treat me unfairly, but I can still stand it and lead a good life!"

Behavioral Effect (E): Loss of anger, relief, and return to the Healthy Negative Consequences: feelings of sorrow and disappointment.

Until you go through these ABC's many, many times, until you do so vigorously, strongly, and powerfully, and until you practice them over and over again, you will tend to sink back into your IBs and back to your Unhealthy Negative Consequences. Only with continual practice will you consistently uproot your IBs and, even then, never for all time to come. You will often tend to return to your former dysfunctional habits—as all humans tend to do. You will hardly attain perfection. But by using the REBT methods, you will tend to recognize your IBs and Unhealthy Negative Consequences. You will improve your Debating and Disputing of your IBs and largely minimize them.

The philosophies of unconditional self-acceptance and unconditional other-acceptance help you realize your own potential as a human while you acknowledge and work at correcting your shortcomings. REBT helps you to judge other people's bad thoughts, feelings, and actions without damning *them* for their unfortunate or obnoxious behaviors. If you want to have little to do with some people when, in your eyes, they behave badly, that of course is your prerogative. But try to think that they *preferably shouldn't* rather than *absolutely shouldn't* act in the ways that you dislike.

9

Feeling Your Way Out of Your Anger

IN THIS CHAPTER we shall discuss some of the emotive methods used in REBT to reduce your anger. By "emotive" we mean forceful, hard-hitting, sometimes dramatic ways of interrupting and changing your anger by focusing on your feelings or desires. "Behavioral" methods, which we consider in the next chapter, may overlap with emotive methods but tend to stress actions rather than feelings. You also tend to use them with less forcefulness or drama.

The first, and perhaps the most important of the emotive methods of overcoming anger and other emotional problems, consists of unconditional self-acceptance. This involves the strong resolve to accept yourself fully, no matter what you may do—including foolishly making yourself enraged!

If you were to come to see us for REBT help, and if you told us that you kept making yourself angry, we would try to show you— by our attitudes and behavior toward you—a good example of what we call *unconditional acceptance*. Thus, we would agree with you about the destructiveness of your anger, but would accept you as a human with this poor behavior and would not in any way put you down. Our acceptance of you despite your behavior might well enable you to accept yourself and to have more time and energy available to change. But even if a therapist doesn't always accept you, in fact even if everyone tends to severely criticize you, you can still accept yourself fully while acting poorly. For if you do take others' criticisms to heart, if you do agree with them that you are a worthless person, you have *decided* to agree with their ideas about you.

Remember!—you can hear your criticizers out, fully acknowledge their negative opinions about you, and then only see your *behavior* as bad but not see yourself as a *bad person* for acting badly. Also, if you already tend to condemn yourself for your bad feelings and actions, you can decide *not* to agree with your own attitudes. You can resolve instead to accept yourself with your failings. This decision, when you make it strongly, is an emotive method of self-choosing.

The more decisively, the more strongly, the more firmly you determine to accept yourself and to refuse to put yourself down, no matter what you do in life, the more you will *feel* self-accepting. You can get this kind of positive feeling by hearing other people's favorable appraisals of you and adopting them as your own. But you can also get it from *choosing* to have it—yes, firmly deciding, *choosing* to accept yourself *with* your failings.

The next step involves your working continually at *maintaining* your feeling of self-acceptance. You believe an idea strongly not merely because it simply occurs to you or because certain people kept repeating it to you but because you *work* at repeating it and proving it over and over again to yourself.

Even if you have a *physically* biased idea, such as the notion that cake tastes good and steak doesn't, you keep repeating this idea to yourself many times, showing yourself—especially when you eat cake—how good it is and how much better than steak. You put a good deal of effort into endorsing one idea ("Cake tastes great!") and verifying an opposing idea ("Steak doesn't taste good!"). Out of this kind of forceful work and practice comes your strong—and highly emotive—conviction about the better taste of cake.

Similarly, you can really practice fully accepting yourself with your rage, if you have it; and the more often and more strongly you work at this acceptance, the better you will feel about yourself. In REBT we assume that anger usually does you more harm than good and that knowing this, you would prefer to reduce it. We see surrendering your IBs as an important part of minimizing anger and enjoying a happier life. At the same time we stress fully accepting yourself while giving up your anger and often repeating to yourself this self-endorsement.

Another emotive technique consists of Rational Emotive Imagery (REI), created by Dr. Maxie C. Maultsby Jr., a rational-behavior psychiatrist. REBT adapts REI as follows:

First, you imagine a negative event or series of events that normally leads to your feeling angry or otherwise upset. Vividly and intensely imagine, for example, that Joan and Jack not only refuse to share the apartment with you and withdraw from their agreement in an inappropriate manner, but also go further by denying that they had ever made such an agreement with you. They strongly assert that you fabricated the whole story in an attempt to manipulate them into sharing an apartment with you.

Now imagine this negative experience, or any experience of your own, that will evoke intense disturbed feelings. Thus, if you think about Jack and Joan going back on their agreement with you and denying that they had ever made such an agreement, you will probably feel quite furious. Rather than avoid your angry or other disturbed feelings, let them erupt with their fullest intensity; let yourself fully *feel* very enraged.

After you have really and truly experienced your rage for a while, push yourself—really try to push yourself—to change these feelings. Use what you have learned from REBT thus far and work through the ABC's step by step. If you feel intense anger, don't think that you can't change this feeling by talking to yourself. You can. You can change your disturbed feelings at almost any time by working at doing so: by getting in touch with your gut-level feeling of anger and by pushing yourself to change so that you experience different and healthier negative feelings, such as those of disappointment and irritation at Joan and Jack's behavior. You definitely have the ability to make these emotional changes. So give it a sincere try; concentrate and do it.

After you have pushed yourself to feel the healthy negative Consequences of disappointment and irritation at what Jack and

Joan are doing to you rather than the feelings of angrily damning *them* for their actions, take a careful look at what you have done to make these changes and try to retrace or recapture the exact steps of your mental process. You will note that you have in some manner changed your Belief System at point B and have thereby changed your emotional Consequences at C. You have probably accomplished this change in your feelings by telling yourself, "Oh, well, I'll never like their going back on and denying we ever had our agreement, but they definitely have a right, as fallible humans, to act that obnoxiously." Or "They really have inconvenienced me greatly by their unfair behavior, but my world won't come to an end because of that inconvenience. How annoying! But I don't have to view it as really all *that* bad."

Let yourself clearly see what you have done by carefully and closely examining what important changes in your Belief System you have made. Make yourself fully aware of the new RBs that create your new healthy negative Consequences (C's) regarding your unpleasant Activating Experiences (A's)—their acting unfairly to you and then denying their unfairness.

If your angry feelings do not change as you attempt to experience healthier feelings, don't give up. Keep fantasizing the same unpleasant experiences or events and keep working at your emotional feelings until you do change them from unhealthy to healthy negative emotions. You create and control your feelings, and you *can* change them.

Once you succeed in feeling disappointed or irritated rather than enraged, and once you see exactly what Beliefs you have changed to make yourself feel bad but not emotionally disturbed, keep repeating the process. Make yourself feel angry, then make yourself feel disappointed and annoyed but not enraged. Then look again at exactly what you did to bring about these changes. Keep practicing by doing this over and over until the process becomes familiar and increasingly less difficult to carry out.

If you keep practicing REI for a few minutes every day for several weeks, you will usually get to a point where, whenever you think of an event about which you would normally make yourself enraged, or whenever this event actually occurs, you will tend automatically to feel healthily disappointed or annoyed rather than unhealthily enraged.

If you have trouble practicing REI every day, you can motivate yourself to practice by rewarding yourself when you do it with some personal pleasure that you particularly enjoy. On days when you fail to do your REI exercise, you can deny yourself something you like or punish yourself by taking up some task you find distasteful.

We have rarely met an individual who could not successfully practice REI to reduce anger. The hundreds of people whom we have encouraged to use this method and who actually and sincerely worked at it have in most cases been able significantly to reduce their tendencies to enrage themselves at many kinds of unfortunate experiences.

You can also employ REI to create pleasurable or good feelings toward people that will divert you from and aid you in overcoming your hostile feelings toward them. R. W. Ramsay, a cognitive-behavior therapist at the University of Amsterdam, has done some experiments in this connection and has worked with a technique he calls emotional training. As applied to anger, you might adapt emotional training as follows:

Think of an intensely pleasant experience you have had with the person with whom you now feel angry. When you have fantasized such a pleasant experience and have actually given yourself un-usually good, intensely warm feelings toward that person as a result of this remembrance, continue the process. Recall pleasant experiences and good feelings, and try to make these feelings paramount over your feelings of hostility.

REI and pleasurable self-training work along the same principles as the hostility-creating self-statements that originally led you to produce your IBs. Left to your own devices, you not only create anger and resentment toward others, but keep practicing and practicing these feelings until they "naturally" or easily keep rising. You may not realize it consciously, but you do this kind of steady practicing when you create unhealthy negative emotions. By the same token, then, you can deliberately practice achieving healthy negative emotions, as you do in REI, or you can deliberately practice feeling positive or pleasurable emotions, as in Ramsay's emotional training technique. You really do have a choice of what you feel, and if you actively use these methods, they can help you experience nonangry feelings.

REBT uses its famous *shame-attacking* and *risk-taking* exercises to help you overcome your feelings of self-hatred, but you can employ them to reduce anger as well. When I (AE) invented these exercises, I realized that most people upset themselves by making themselves feel ashamed: ashamed of doing something wrong and ashamed of others' witnessing their wrongdoing and thinking poorly of them. Using REBT, we try to get clients to do things that they consider risky, shameful, embarrassing, or humiliating, such as telling strangers that they have just been released from a mental institution, yelling out the time of day in public, or wearing outlandish clothing. They then can see that these "shameful" acts really didn't make them feel embarrassed or lead to self-hatred unless they themselves *decided* to feel that way. They can also see that the acts often do not make others despise them as the "shamed" people think they will. Others quickly forget about these acts, and rarely overconcern themselves about them. If you feel terribly ashamed or embarrassed by various harmless acts—like singing in public—you can try a few of them until you see that not only can you bear to do them, but you can also help yourself become much less prone to embarrassment. And you can even come to enjoy some of them!

At times you may cover up your feelings of shame or embarrassment with anger. You can use the shame-attacking method described above to undo feeling ashamed and angry. For example, suppose a waiter in a high-class restaurant gives you poor service and you feel ashamed to complain about it for fear that he will treat you with disdain or perhaps make some loud disparaging remarks about you. Force yourself to speak unangrily to the waiter about the poor service and even ask him to do something you normally wouldn't ask for, for instance, that he replace your soup, which you find too cold, with warmer soup. By doing this, you will see that it really has no intrinsic "shamefulness." As you do it, also try to get yourself to see that the waiter has his own fallibility and that once you express your displeasure with his behavior, you do not have to condemn him for it.

Similarly, if you tend to feel hostile toward people who appear to act unfriendly to you, go out of your way "shamefully" to encounter some of them: horn in on a conversation they are having with someone else, or insist that you have met them before when you really haven't. By working against your shame, you will probably see that you invent some of people's "unfriendliness" as a protection against your feeling ashamed to encounter them.

Risk-taking and shame-attacking exercises of this type are assertive actions. This brings us to regular assertion training, which REBT has used since its inception and which constitutes an excellent way to prevent or tone down feelings of anger. For just as anger frequently stems from feelings of shame, it also frequently stems from deep-seated feelings of unassertiveness. You would like, for example, to say no to a friend's request that you have no desire to fulfill, yet you don't feel comfortable about asserting yourself in this situation. Perhaps you fear being rejected if you don't agree, so you withhold your feelings and go along with your friend's wishes. But because you are unassertive, you can easily hate yourself for acting so weakly and for making yourself incensed at your friend for "manipulating" you.

If your unassertiveness leads to rage, you can give this up by training yourself to act more assertively. Thus, if you firmly keep refusing to go along with individuals who try to get you to do so, you will not act weakly, will have no reason to condemn yourself, and will avoid condemning others for forcing you to do what you do not want to do.

Assertion training, though it falls under behavioral methods of combating anger (which we will consider in the next chapter) is also an emotive technique. If you sincerely want to say no to someone but say yes because you fear rejection, you can force yourself to say no until you naturally feel good while holding your ground.

Forcing yourself to behave differently from the way you usually do comprises the main emotive element here. As we keep noting, "emotional" thinking and "emotional" activity are strong, forceful, biased behaviors. When emotional, you greatly want things to go a certain way, and you feel highly motivated to get what you want or avoid what you don't want. Emotionally, you move *powerfully* toward or away from various people and conditions. By the same token, forcing yourself to change your behavior (especially when you have trouble doing so) is an emotive, dramatic form of self-modification. Assertion training frequently consists of this kind of emotional commitment.

In REBT we have always employed some of the role-playing and behavior-rehearsal techniques originally created by J. L. Moreno and then adapted by Fritz Perls and the Gestalt therapists. Whereas Moreno, Perls, and others tend to use these techniques largely for catharsis—for the reliving of early emotional experiences—we tend to use them in more behavioral ways.

Suppose, for example, that you want to firmly but unangrily confront someone and you have trouble doing so. The leader of your therapy group might get you to try to express the feelings you have about this situation. You might then role-play yourself, and another member of your group might role-play the part of the person whom you wish to confront. You might then do this confronting and the members of your therapy group might give a critique of your presentation, commenting on whether you spoke (1) too hesitantly; (2) too honestly; (3) with distinct hostility instead of assertiveness; or (4) quite appropriately. If you did well, they might ask you to repeat the performance several times to improve it and get used to it. If you did poorly, they might ask you to try doing it again in several different ways until you not only expressed what you felt but also did so in a way that would most likely bring you the results you wanted.

When alone, you can do this kind of role-playing or emotive acting out in your head, in front of a mirror, or with the use of a tape recorder. Or you can do it with the help of a friend or a group of friends. It does not require a therapist or a therapy group, though often you will find such a setting useful, just as you would find it useful to practice acting in a play in front of a teacher and a group of fellow actors.

You employ REBT-type role-playing, either with yourself or with others, not merely to express yourself and your feelings or to let off steam, but to show yourself that you really create your own feelings of anger and that you have much better choices. Many kinds of psychotherapies believe that if you feel angry at someone or something, you have to let out this anger before you can deal with the situation sensibly. You then might find yourself screaming or yelling loudly at someone, pounding pillows (which may represent the person you would wish to strike), or otherwise "letting out" your anger.

As we showed in chapter 2, considerable clinical and experimental evidence indicates that the more you take out your anger in the above manner, the angrier you will tend to become. REBT offers a good explanation for this occurrence. If you, for example, deliberately insult someone who has done something wrong to you or if you pound on a pillow that represents that person, you in all probability tell yourself something like, "He really did treat me unfairly and I hate him. He *should not* have acted that way toward me, and I really hope that he gets this type of treatment back twice as much as he gave it to me!"

As you express your feelings in this manner, you will confirm your irrational ideas about the person you think has abused you. "She has acted 100 percent wrongly." "She had no right whatsoever to make such mistakes." "She is a rotten person for acting in that way." "She deserves to get punished." Perhaps after you release your hostility in this active manner, you will go back and review what actually happened and somewhat forgive the other person for her "awful" acts. More than likely, however, your expressed hostility will only serve to help you exacerbate the "terribleness" of acts of those you hate and make you feel, for the present and the future, even angrier at them.

Some individuals, after physically or verbally expressing their hostility to others (or to the world), see how much they keep making a mountain out of a molehill, and then calm down and feel only disappointed and sorry about the way others treat them. But the majority of people seem to confirm their irrational view that others *absolutely shouldn't* act badly toward them and that bad acts mean that the entire person is bad. Ironically, the more these people release, ventilate or "abreact" (re-feel and reenact some earlier experiences of) their anger, the angrier they feel, and the more likely they are to make themselves angry again at future unfairnesses. So although occasionally in REBT we help people express their pent-up feelings of anger (for example, by forcing themselves to tell someone off in one of our group or marathon therapy sessions) and although we help them show their feelings of annoyance or displeasure at the behavior of other people, as stated previously, we almost always try to help them see that they really create their own feelings of anger and that they have much better choices.

REBT emphasizes that when you feel others treat you unfairly, you had better acknowledge your feelings of anger, if you have them, admit that you foolishly created these feelings, and surrender your shoulds and musts with which you created them. In this way, you can end up feeling very disappointed and sorry rather than angry, and you can perhaps choose to express these healthy negative feelings instead of choosing to express your unhealthy hostile feelings.

REBT by no means objects to your having intense feelings, including negative ones, but instead encourages you fully to acknowledge, get in touch with, and stop denying such feelings. It shows you how to discriminate healthy feelings of annoyance and displeasure from unhealthy feelings of anger and rage. It teaches you how to keep the former, how to change the latter. It gives you a choice about whether—and how—you express your feelings to others. No matter how you feel, you'd better honestly recognize your feelings. But recognize doesn't necessarily mean endorse. Nor does it mean express. Some of your authentic feelings you can fully endorse and had better express. But not all of them!

10

Acting Your Way Out of Your Anger

LIKE FEELINGS OF PLEASURE, emotional disturbance involves active repetition. You *practice* feeling upset and after a while automatically feel that way.

In the case of anger, you often "saw" people treat you "unfairly" during your childhood and told yourself something like: "They must not treat me so unfairly!" You then made yourself feel angry and lashed back at them.

Over a period of time, as you "practiced" and "practiced" this IB, you easily and automatically began to Believe that you *absolutely must* receive "fair" treatment, and you made it part of your basic philosophy. Thus, when you start with the observation, "They treated me unfairly," and you add the RB "as I wish they wouldn't," you feel healthily sorry and disappointed. When you add the IB, "They must not treat me so unfairly!" you usually make yourself feel furious.

REBT shows you that when you acquire the *habit* of feeling and acting angrily you also have the underlying *habit* of thinking irrationally. So if you want to change your behavioral habit, you'd better also change your thinking habit. The two go together.

But REBT also shows you that just as your thoughts influence your feelings and behaviors, the latter also greatly affect your thinking. Why? Because that's the way humans are wired: They behave according to their thoughts—*and* they think according to their behaviors.

Suppose, for example, you have a difficult time learning to play tennis because you feel inferior and put yourself down for not making any progress at mastering the game. You can—in spite of your negative attitudes—force yourself to play daily no matter how poorly you perform. Although your self-defeating views and feelings of inferiority will probably interfere with your learning to play well, they probably won't make you unable to play the game at all.

Despite your feelings and your tendencies to withdraw, you may persist at practicing this sport. As you do so, you ultimately play tennis better, and finally, you may begin to play quite well. You now *see* that you *can* play well. You get a Belief and a feeling of what Albert Bandura calls self-efficacy.

By forcing yourself—in spite of your attitudes—to keep practicing tennis, you can actually have an effect on your negative attitudes and give up your disturbance about tennis. You can probably do this more thoroughly and efficiently if you also work at finding and Disputing your IBs that you *must* play tennis well and that you are an inferior person if you don't. But just as your Beliefs influence your behavior, your behavior also influences your Beliefs. You therefore have a choice of working on changing both your beliefs and your behavior or of changing either one to help you change the other.

REBT encourages you to make both these choices. It not only uses thinking and feeling methods, as shown in our previous chapters, but it also pushes you to employ a number of active-directive, behavioral methods. Thus, it has pioneered and acquired some degree of fame in promoting active, *in vivo* (in your own life) homework assignments. This means that we give our regular clients—and we can teach people like you to give yourself—steady homework assignments to assist them in overcoming their emotional problems.

Using our previous illustration, let us assume that you feel angry at Joan and Jack for withdrawing from your agreement and that you seek help from an REBT therapist. Your first homework assignment might consist of your maintaining contact with them while you keep working through your problems of anger. For if you immediately break off contact because of the anger you feel toward them, your withdrawal will be something of a cop-out.

Your first goal may be your stopping Jack and Joan from continuing to treat you unfairly—which you can easily do if you discontinue your relationship with them. But you also want to make yourself feel only healthily disappointed or annoyed with their actions rather than unhealthily enraged at *them*. So if you merely discontinue relationships with them (and others who "make" you angry), you will have done nothing to improve your *own* behavior and feelings. *You* still are stirring yourself up!

As we noted before, your avoiding "unjust" persons and situations does nothing to alter your anger-creating philosophy. You still have it, and you will continue to use it to enrage yourself whenever other negative Activating Experiences occur. If, however, you give yourself the homework assignment of continuing to stay in some kind of relationship with people who have treated you unjustly, and if you *still* don't anger yourself about what they have done to you, then you can really work on, and to a considerable degree change, your anger-creating Irrational Beliefs.

Your homework assignment can consist of two distinct parts: first, your activity itself (maintaining contact with Jack and Joan) and second, your thinking (changing your ideas about Joan and Jack while you remain in contact with them). REBT favors homework assignments that are both behavioral and philosophical because by using this dual approach, you can work through your emotional and behavioral problems simultaneously and learn by your own thoughts and actions how to reduce your rage.

In many situations anxiety accompanies anger. You often make yourself angry because you feel anxious about confronting others with their poor or unfair behavior, and by angering yourself you cover up the feeling of helplessness that often accompanies your anxiety. Thus, you may use anger to create the false sense that you are really doing something about an unjust situation.

In vivo or live homework assignments can help you work out these related difficulties of anger, anxiety, and depression in several ways. As mentioned, one of them involves your staying in an unpleasant situation and working through your disturbed feelings about it. For example, if you feel anxious about confronting Joan and Jack about their unfair treatment, you can force yourself to confront them about a number of lesser faults you think they have. You may mention such things as their failure to meet or call you when they agreed to do so or their being very critical of you. Because you thereby already have started discussing unpleasant topics, you may find it easier to work up to discussing the unfairness issue without feeling so anxious.

You can also try dealing with your feelings of self-blame about having your anger. You can force yourself to realize that you have a right, as a human, to have feelings of anger. Thus, if you had a temper tantrum privately against Joan and Jack, you could while acknowledging the foolishness of this tantrum still accept yourself as an okay person. In this frame of mind you would find it far easier to dispute your IBs, for you would allow yourself to see that you have them without calling yourself a stupid person.

These behavioral homework assignments can help you face disturbing experiences and deal with them rationally. You thereby see that you can survive happily in spite of your frustrations. In acquiring the discipline these assignments demand, you tend to increase your frustration tolerance. This helps you because emotional disturbances—anger, anxiety, depression—often stem from low frustration tolerance (LFT). You may remain anxious about confronting someone because you refuse to bear the discomfort you would feel while confronting her or him.

Good homework assignments can help you stay with unpleasant situations and tolerate them until you can effectively change them. They also help you take on present pains for future gains, as when you force yourself to confront people quickly about their unfairness in order to induce them to treat you more considerately. The more you do this kind of REBT homework, the more you tend to increase your tolerance for frustration and thereby minimize your tendencies to make yourself angry and depressed.

REBT also makes use of B. F. Skinner's technique of reinforcement or operant conditioning. This self-management technique bases itself on the principles of reward and punishment. You carry out conditioning by rewarding yourself with a prize (such as food, approval, or another pleasure) when you perform a desired behavior and with a penalty when you do not perform it.

Using penalties, as well as reinforcements or rewards, isn't the same thing as damning and putting yourself down for your poor behavior. Quite the contrary! You penalize yourself for undesirable actions to *help* yourself change them. But damning yourself for "bad" actions may actually push you into doing more of them.

Skinner's work has often led to considerable criticism because a behavior therapist can manipulate people by using reinforcing principles to get them to do things they don't really want to do. Authorities can abuse the technique, especially in controlled environments such as schools, hospitals, and prisons. As used in REBT, however, operant conditioning mainly consists of contingency management or self-control procedures. Clients who wish to change their self-defeating behaviors and, particularly, to discipline themselves in various ways that they normally find difficult agree to engage in certain assignments and to engage in pleasant reinforcements only if they complete these assignments satisfactorily. They also agree to accept certain penalties if they do not carry out their assignments.

Self-management principles also apply to individuals who make contracts with themselves. Writers and artists have for many centuries helped themselves work at their crafts for a minimum period of time each day by allowing themselves to eat, read, or talk to their friends only after they have put in this allotted time. Millions of people have induced themselves to diet, exercise, or do other unpleasant tasks by imposing some stiff penalty on themselves if they do not live up to the contracts they make with themselves.

To apply contingency management to REBT, let us say that you have trouble spending time every day working on Disputing your irrational beliefs and doing other homework assignments. You can make a contract with yourself, and perhaps can write your agreement down in clear terms. As a reward (or reinforcement) for carrying out your exercises, you can select any activity you particularly enjoy. Each day that you spend the required time doing your homework, you can reward yourself. Failure to meet the requirements of your contract may lead you to penalize yourself (with some activity you find highly distasteful).

You may sometimes seek the help of another person to assist you in enforcing this contract. A close friend or associate will often happily supervise you as you reward or penalize yourself. An arrangement of this nature helps ensure that your penalties and rewards are faithfully enforced—a crucial aspect of contingency management.

Because people have such a wide range of likes and dislikes, we shall not suggest specific rewards and penalties. In general, rewards had better be practical and available. Thus, if you reward yourself by having sex with a partner every time you do your homework, your partner may not find this act so rewarding! And you may get tired of it yourself!

Like rewards, devise penalties within reason. Too severe or hard-to-enforce penalties do little good. A penalty can be depriving yourself of reading or of TV. Or it can add a burden to your life, such as eating food you dislike.

If you wish, you can institute a special reward and penalty system. If you do your homework every day of the week, for instance, you can give yourself a super reward on the weekend—such as going to dinner at a special restaurant. If you haven't kept your homework agreement, you can impose a big penalty, like having to get up an hour early for a whole week.

Let us reiterate the difference between penalties and self-damnation. You may decide to penalize laboratory animals for going down the wrong pathways in a maze in order to help them discover the right pathways. But you certainly wouldn't scream at or brutalize them if they don't respond correctly.

So long as you stay with the idea "I *want* to give up my anger," you can logically follow it with: "And since I find it so hard to give it up and so difficult to work against it, I *want* to find a penalty that will help me work at reducing it." If you use this kind of formula, your desire to accept the penalty outweighs your desire to avoid the difficult task of disciplining yourself to change your anger. You willingly impose a penalty on yourself in order to overcome your unwillingness to accept the pain of the self-discipline.

When you damn rather than penalize yourself, however, you really tell yourself, "I *must* give up my anger and make myself do my homework! If I don't do what I *must* do, I not only will penalize myself, but will also put myself down for not keeping my agreement with myself." Your self-agreement includes a destructive *must* and a self-damning consequence of that *must*. Change your *must* to a *preference* and rid yourself of your damning!

As we noted before, REBT also employs a good deal of assertion training to help people act assertively rather than aggressively. When you assert yourself, you merely seek what you want and avoid what you don't want. When you act aggressively, however, you also add anger to your feelings and acts—by your Belief that others have *no right* to block you from getting what you want, and your Belief that they therefore are *rotten people*. REBT teaches you how to distinguish assertion from aggression and how to firmly strive for the things you want without hating others, antagonizing them, refusing to compromise, and demanding that they absolutely must give you everything you desire. For, as a number of studies have shown, learning to be assertive results in significant anger reduction.

REBT philosophically sets the stage for your being assertive rather than aggressive. Once you understand the REBT principle that others do not *make you* angry but that you largely create your own hostile feelings, you can proceed to do assertion training exercises that will help you overcome a good deal of your rage and fury.

Self-assertion involves the risk-taking actions of doing what you really want to do and refraining from doing what you really don't want to do. Naturally, other people may think badly of you for your assertiveness, so you had better consider its possible penalties before you assert yourself—particularly when you do so with a supervisor, boss, or other person with power. You then may deem the risks you take too high, and decide not to assert yourself. Deliberately holding back may at times constitute very rational behavior!

Often, however, when you behave passively you view normal risk-taking as being *too* risky because you are overconcerned about losing the approval of other people. You may have to risk disapproval, however, in order to allow yourself the freedom to ask for what you want. First, observe and question your avoidances, and then practice making more assertive moves.

Some common assertive homework assignments that we would encourage you to try in REBT include the following:

Take specific risks. Think of a few things you would like to do but have usually felt extremely afraid to do and have therefore avoided, like sending back a poorly cooked dish in a restaurant. Or wearing an article of clothing that looks rather flashy. Or eating a sandwich when riding a bus or subway train. Or raising your hand in a large audience to ask what people may view as a foolish question. Or unangrily telling someone that you dislike his or her behavior.

Risk rejection by asking for something. Think of something you really want, such as sex, a special food, a back rub, or going to a movie—something you think will result in a cold or angry refusal if you ask for it. Risk it by specifically asking one of your associates or friends for this thing. When you get refused, still try to talk the other person into acquiescing. If you don't succeed, try again later to get what you want.

Risk saying no. Pick something that you don't usually want to do but that you often do in order to please others, such as going out to eat, having sex in a certain way, or carrying on a conversation for a long period of time—and deliberately take the risk of refusing to do this thing. You can at times nastily refuse, just to make the risk of saying no greater. Or, better, you can nicely but firmly refuse, and persist at refusing, even though the other person keeps trying to get you to do what he or she wants.

Do something ridiculous or "shameful."   As noted in the previous chapter, you can do some shame-attacking exercises. Think of something you would think foolish to do in public and deliberately do this "shameful" or "embarrassing" thing. Like singing at the top of your lungs in the street. Or walking a banana, as if you were walking a dog or a cat, on a ribboned leash. Or wearing a headband with a large yellow feather stuck in it. Or stopping a little old lady and asking if she would help you cross the street.

Deliberately show that you have failed at an important task.   Make yourself fail at a worthy project and make sure that a number of people know about your failure. While playing in a baseball game, for example, deliberately drop a flyball that practically falls into your hands. During a public speech make yourself stutter for a while. Tell people that you have failed at an examination when you have really passed it.

Assert yourself coolly.   Some advocates of assertion training swear by the fight-'em-and-assert-yourself plan and forget that playing it cool often is a better way of getting what you want. If you feel angry toward someone and see that you—and not him or her—created your anger, you can work on reducing your rage and coolly instead of furiously disagree with this person.

As Lois Bird correctly points out when offering advice as to how to get along better with one's partner, "I don't care what you feel on a gut level; you don't have to spread it all over the verbal landscape. You can turn it off and talk to [your mate] with your cool intact." Follow Bird's advice and you will usually be more effectively assertive than if you "honestly" tell your partner off.

Courageous confrontation.   As noted above, hostility and violence often stem from lack of courage. You refuse to go after what you want or to confront others with their lapses. Then, hating yourself for your own weakness, you feel angry and combative toward those with whom you have acted weakly.

Instead, you can courageously confront those with whom you disagree. Often, conflict will occur, but at least you will put things out in the open, and resolution sooner or later may result. If, therefore, you will courageously confront those with whom you seriously disagree and refrain from making yourself angry and violent, your confronting may show them that you have little fear, will try to sensibly prevail, and deserve consideration and perhaps compromise.

How do you do this kind of direct confrontation? By convincing yourself that you can stand opposition and rudeness and that even if others dislike you, you never need dislike yourself. You then can fairly easily force yourself—yes, force yourself!—to confront your opponents. No matter what your initial pain of so doing, remember that the pain of avoidance generally is much worse—and lasts much longer!

Role-playing. Robert Alberti and Michael Emmons explain in detail how therapists can help their clients, especially their marital counseling clients, by role-playing with them assertive rather than aggressive behavior. You can do the same thing without a therapist by having one of your friends role-play a mock fight between you and, say, your mate or your boss. Set up a specific scene of conflict. Decide with your onlooker exactly what the two of you, you and your antagonist, will do. Have onlookers criticize your role-playing. Replay the "drama." Then have more feedback and coaching by your onlookers. Repeat the role-playing several times. You can also record your role-playing and listen to it a few times.

Prior preparation. Assertion, as George Bach and Herb Goldberg point out, often consists of preparing yourself in advance to deal with passive aggressors or procrastinators. Thus, one of your friends may promise to meet you for appointments and never show up or consistently turn up late. If so, you then set very precise and active rules, such as "If you don't show up by ten-thirty and I haven't heard from you by phone, I shall go to the movies by myself." In making these rules, make sure that you don't make them idly and that you really stick to them.

Clearly distinguish assertion from aggression.   Alberti and Emmons make a fine point of clearly distinguishing assertive from aggressive behavior, following some prior leads by Arnold Lazarus and my own (AE's) writings. As Arnold Lazarus and Allen Fay wrote, "Assertion involves taking a stand, resisting unreasonable demands, or asking for what you want. Aggression involves putting another person down. Assertion is positive, aggression negative." The main differences among unassertive, assertive, and aggressive behavior include the following:

Unassertive behavior: You want something and do not honestly express your want or make any real effort to obtain it. You resort to indirect, passive, somewhat dishonest actions. You frequently do not admit to yourself what you really want and don't want. You needlessly inhibit yourself and even deny some of your basic desires. You tend to feel anxious, hurt, and angry.

Assertive behavior: You want something, honestly acknowledge to yourself that you want it, and for the most part try to get it. You tend to act openly with others, though sometimes you do not fully reveal to them what you want but persistently try to obtain it. You feel self-interested and self-enhancing. You respect other people's values and goals but often prefer your own to theirs. You behave actively and expressively.

Aggressive behavior: You feel angry toward others for blocking your goals and often try to do them in rather than to get what you want. You strongly believe that they should not, must not thwart you. You are emotionally honest but in an inappropriate way, often interfering with what you really want from others or with others. You behave actively and assertively but at the expense of others. You express yourself fully—and frequently overdo it. You often feel righteous and superior to others and tend to damn them. You may also feel guilty about your hostility.

If you will clearly distinguish among these three kinds of behavior and not merely assume you only have a choice between unassertiveness and aggression, you can train yourself to act truly assertively, and be responsible toward both yourself and others— as Arthur Lange and Patricia Jakubowski and other REBT-oriented therapists advocate.

Acting assertively. Some of the elements of acting assertively, as outlined by Lange and Jakubowski and by Janet L. Wolfe, include these behaviors:

- When expressing your desire not to do something, use a decided no. Don't hedge or leave the decision up to the other person. Don't make yourself defensive or apologetic.
- Speak in an audible, firm tone of voice. Avoid whining, harsh, and accusatory statements.
- Give as prompt and brief a reply as possible, without using long pauses or interruptions.
- Try to have others treat you with fairness and justice and point out when they don't. But don't insist or command!
- When asked to do something you consider unreasonable, ask for an explanation and listen to it carefully. Where appropriate, suggest an alternative act or solution you would rather use.
- Honestly express your feelings without using evasion, attacking the other person, or trying to justify yourself in a defensive manner.
- When expressing displeasure or annoyance, try to tell the other person specifically what you dislike. Don't attack the person, name-call, or imply that he or she deserves some kind of damnation!
- Recognize the usefulness of I-messages instead of you-messages, but also note that the former provide no panacea. Some advocates of assertion training advocate I-messages and the use of anger in the learning of assertiveness. But therapists like Arnold Lazarus and David D. Hewes point out that I-messages, too, can include unhealthy rage while appropriate you-messages may not. Thus, if you object to the way a salesman acts, you can angrily

say, with an I-message, "I feel really miffed when I try to buy a shirt from you and you behave the way you do." Or you can unangrily, with a you-message, say, "You really seem to feel uptight today. I really like your low-pressure approach better." Lazarus, when using a you-message, includes an understanding of the other person and even a positive reinforcement of him or her. So use but don't overvalue I-messages.

Degrees of assertiveness.   Marlowe H. Smaby and Armas W. Tamminen point out that various degrees of assertiveness exist and that some of them are appropriate for different kinds of situations or with different partners. Using minimal assertiveness, you merely hold your ground and refuse to let another control you—as when someone tries to horn in on a line ahead of you and you merely point to the back of the line and indicate that he or she had better go to it.

Using the next level of acting confidently assertive, you recognize another's side of an issue and his feelings about it, but without vindictiveness you solidly hold your ground. Thus, if a friend wants you to lie for him, you say, "I can see how you feel about this and why you want me to do this and how disappointed you will feel if I don't. But I also have strong feelings that I don't want to do this and will possibly get into some kind of trouble, so I wish you wouldn't ask me to do it. In fact, I feel somewhat uneasy about it now that you have asked."

Using a higher level, bargaining assertiveness, you still firmly hold your ground but also go out of your way to see the other's point of view and make some kind of compromise solution. Thus, you may say to the friend who wants you to lie, "I can see how you feel about this and why you want me to do what you want and how disappointed you will feel if I don't. But I also have strong feelings that I don't want to do this and will possibly get into some kind of trouble, so you can see how I feel about it and why I won't do it. But I think I can see another way to help you. I will stick pretty much to the truth but will really go out of my way to get that employer to give you a job so that he can see how capable you are. I will recommend that he give it to you even though you may lack the experience he desires."

If you practice these different levels of assertion and use them discriminatingly, you can act the way you want to act and still remain on good terms—even very friendly terms—with others.

If you take these assertive risks as you practice REBT, you won't feel ashamed and you won't condemn yourself for acting in a way that at times seems foolish. Your goal in REBT doesn't consist of taking social risks or of bucking conventions simply for the sake of doing so. You stress the gains you can make by your risk-taking. When you take risks without worrying too much what other people may think of you, you assert yourself while at the same time convincing yourself that nothing *horrible* will happen. Also, you keep learning that you can tolerate the disapproval of others although you may not particularly like it. You feel that no person, including yourself, can legitimately put *you* down or evaluate *you* as a rotten person when you perform an unpopular *act*.

We are not saying that you will automatically surrender all your angry feelings and actions and become an individual who feels healthily displeased but never enraged when certain unpleasant things occur. For even if you consistently act assertively, you may still remain an injustice collector who not only easily finds things wrong but also whines and screams when unfair things happen. We still hold that you often create your anger by acting passively and unassertively. And if you practice assertion—while realizing that you do not need the approval of other people—you will tend to less frequently make yourself angry.

REBT stresses education and, consequently, employs many educational methods, including reading materials, audiovisual aids, charts and diagrams, slogans, and *modeling*. If you saw me (RCT) as a therapist and presented your problem of enraging yourself at people who treat you unfairly, I would try to model REBT's antianger philosophy for you. Thus, if you came late to therapy sessions, failed to listen to what I kept saying to you, refused to do your homework assignments, or otherwise showed resistance to learning and changing, I would attempt to *show you that I definitely disliked your behavior but that I did not angrily condemn you for displaying that behavior.*

Not that I would necessarily show complete calm or indifference to such actions. I most probably wouldn't! I take my work as a therapist very seriously, and if you failed to listen, for instance, I would still emphatically try to get you to see your self-defeating philosophies (your IBs) and would try to teach you how to uproot them. I would not angrily condemn you for failing to listen.

I would not want you to develop an emotional dependence on me and to change yourself because I wanted you to do so. As mentioned previously, when you openly criticize others for their outrageous behavior you often encourage them to *defend* that same behavior, thereby exerting their right to it. They might not feel they have to hold on to their offensive behavior if you allowed them to think about it on their own. Thus, they might change their behavior for themselves. Similarly, as your therapist, I would try to help you to change for your own benefit and not for mine. To do this, I would behave as a good model for you to follow—as someone who provided you with contrast, someone who showed you more about your irrational behavior (anger) through that contrast.

Without any therapist to serve as a rational model, how could you get this kind of benefit? Answer: by finding good models in your own life. Unfortunately, most people whom you encounter hardly fall into this category. In fact, they may often anger themselves about trivial injustices as well as about important ones. Exceptions, however, do exist, like an unusual friend or teacher, an occasional relative, an associate—people who feel determined to overcome life's unniceties and who actively keep working at doing so.

Talk to these people.

Try to learn from them how they manage to keep reasonably cool in the face of real injustices. Observe them in action. See if you can model some of your own feelings and behaviors after theirs. Find them in books and other biographical materials, for literature is full of figures who suffered great frustrations and even persecutions without making themselves unduly enraged or homicidal. Seek out these rational models and learn about their lives.

There are a number of other behavioral methods of working against anger that REBT finds effective. These are briefly described below.

Exposure to hostility. Exposure to hostility, in the course of group therapy, in a self-help group, or in your regular life, may help you. This does not mean that the hostility *itself* changes you, for it frequently serves as a bad model. But if you practice *coping* with people's hostility, especially under therapeutic supervision, you may well help yourself handle it more effectively and to look closer at and understand the nature of your own rage. As mentioned earlier, avoiding a bad situation often leaves your angry feelings unresolved. Exposing yourself to angry people while *not* upsetting yourself may work much better.

Constructive activities. As Andrew S. Wachtel and Martha Penn Davis and many other researchers have indicated, angry and violent individuals tend to feel alienated, anonymous, and impersonal. If they—and you!—can experience devotion to a highly constructive group or cause, they—and you—may divert themselves from their sense of alienation and anonymity and from their anger.

Early conditioning. Victor Denenberg and M. J. Zarrow did a series of fascinating experiments involving newborn mice, contrasting one group raised by rats with a control group raised by mice. They found "the mice reared by rats were heavier than the mouse-raised control mice. They also were less active in the open field and preferred to spend time near a rat instead of near a mouse. One most dramatic finding was that the rat-reared mice would *not* fight when placed in a standard fighting-box situation." This was in contrast to the occurrence of a great many fights among the control mice reared by mice mothers, thus showing that the "natural" tendency of mice to fight can be significantly altered by having them "unnaturally" reared.

Other experimenters have found that mice raised in close proximity to dogs or cats will not later get attacked by these natural enemies, while mice raised regularly will be attacked. Denenberg and Zarrow say "We must therefore reject any hypothesis that states that aggression is a genetically determined, instinctive response that cannot be modified by experience.... This is not to suggest that genetic factors are not important. It is obvious that they are. What we are saying is that *both the genetic background and the environment in which those genes grow and develop must be considered* jointly *if we are to advance our understanding of behavior patterns.*"

From this information it seems likely that humans subjected to early conditioning designed to lessen their anger may also reduce their natural biological tendencies to act angrily and violently. Naturally, you can now do little about your own childhood, but you could give some thought, if you have children, to helping condition them to act with less hostility.

Distraction measures. As noted above, constructive action may serve as a good diversion from hostility, and so may less constructive behaviors. Norman Zinberg, following the ideas of William James and Sigmund Freud, wonders whether some kinds of competitive activities, such as organized sports and politics, will more successfully serve as forms of sublimation for anger and violence than other kinds of activities, such as movies or private enterprise. As mentioned in chapter 2 the *REBT position assumes that highly aggressive pursuits, such as dog-eat-dog business competition and prizefighting, help make people more rather than less hostile in their feelings and behaviors.*

Robert Barton and Paul Bell found that mild degrees of sexual arousal served to inhibit subsequent physical aggression. As noted in our next chapter, the use of relaxation techniques also tends to reduce feelings of anger. From the evidence available, it would appear that several kinds of enjoyable, constructive, and even neutral distractions can interfere with and at least temporarily ease hostility. Consequently, if you want to control your own angry feelings, you can use such distractions, either to help you temporarily reduce your anger or to give you time to change your thinking so that you make yourself feel less enraged when confronted with obnoxious stimuli in the future. As distractions, you can use thoughts, fantasies, games, activities, emotional involvements, pleasures, or any number of other intense concentrations.

Experiment and discover what particularly works for you in this regard. Keep in mind, however, that unless you change your self-angering thoughts, your rage will likely return once your distractions end.

Coping and problem-solving procedures.   One of the main factors that seems to help almost all kinds of disturbed emotional reactions consists of your consciously engaging in effective coping procedures. In fact, learning effective problem-solving skills has been shown in several studies to lead to significant anger reduction. These studies are summarized in the book edited by Howard Kassinove, *Anger Disorders: Definition, Diagnosis, and Treatment.*

Try, therefore, to develop a good set of coping measures to use when you encounter obnoxious situations and badly behaving people. To do this, list all the unfortunate events that you think will arise with a difficult person or situation and all the possible actions you can take—no matter how good or bad they may be—to cope with the problems you have listed. Then try to figure out the (good and bad) consequences of each action you may take. Be as accurate as you can about your predictions. Then pick the best actions you have planned, follow them through, and keep revising them according to the actual results you achieve with them.

If, by following your coping plans, you come to know that you can deal fairly well with difficult persons or situations, you will have less of a tendency to enrage yourself about them. This is not an ideal solution—because you will not cope effectively with every troublesome situation. But detailed coping plans will help in many instances.

Cognitive restructuring homework.   REBT homework includes many cognitive, emotive, and behavioral methods—that is, much practice in between sessions if you are in therapy and much practice by yourself if you are using REBT self-help techniques. Cognitive restructuring, or finding and Disputing your IBs that spark and maintain your anger, is one of the most useful exercises you can keep practicing.

Raymond Novaco's pioneering study showed that cognitive restructuring, as originated by REBT and by Donald Meichenbaum, worked better than relaxation methods in helping people reduce their anger, and Jerry Deffenbacher and his colleagues at Colorado State University, as well as several other researchers, showed in a series of treatment studies that people can significantly cut down their anger by becoming aware of and actively changing their rage-related Beliefs.

We find the same thing in regular sessions of REBT. We first show clients how they philosophically create their feelings of anger—by whining about injustices and frustrations and demanding that these absolutely must not exist. We then show them how to relax, how to use several REBT anger-coping methods, and how otherwise to live with and minimize their rage.

By using REBT techniques, you can do the same thing for yourself. Acknowledge fully that you create your own enraged feelings and see how you do so—by insisting and commanding that something exist when it doesn't or that something must not exist when it unquestionably does. As you understand this and work to surrender your own commands on others and on the universe, you will find yourself more able to employ the various behavioral methods that we have outlined in this chapter.

Let us emphasize once again that although REBT has a distinct theory of human nature, of emotional disturbance, and of effective psychotherapy and although it uses many therapeutic techniques, it is an integrative rather than an eclectic therapy. It covers, in some respects, over fifty cognitive, emotive, and behavioral methods, many of which differ greatly from one another. But it uses them because they appropriately fall under its main theories of emotional disturbance and change.

Its behavioral methods, for example, do not merely consist of symptom removal. If an REBT therapist persuades you to employ several behavioral techniques—such as activity homework assignments, operant conditioning, and assertion training—to help you reduce your anger, she will not do so merely to encourage you to stop feeling angry right now, while you remain in therapy. No. She will try to see that you leave therapy understanding how you incite yourself to anger, how you can reduce this in the future as well as in the present, and how you can minimize your anger under any set of difficult conditions that may later plague you.

By giving you theoretical understanding and practical techniques that you can employ yourself, REBT provides you with a treatment method that will enable you not only to *feel* better, but to *get* better—and preferably to make yourself less disturbed *and* less disturb*able*. It helps you, if you are willing to work at it, to make a profound philosophical and emotional change that will hopefully encourage you to think, feel, and act less self-defeatingly and more enjoyably for the rest of your days.

11

Learning to Relax

AS DESCRIBED IN CHAPTER 1, anger mentally and physically prepares you to confront danger. While your thinking creates much of your anger, physical arousal and agitation can fuel it and keep it going. Consequently, learning to calm yourself down physically is an important tool you can use to interrupt and reduce your rage.

You can choose a number of techniques to reduce your tension and arousal, including progressive muscle relaxation, guided imagery, autogenic training, biofeedback, and various forms of meditation. If used properly and steadily, these methods can lead to positive changes in your body, such as decreases in heart rate, blood pressure, and muscle tension. With practice, you can learn to relax your body as soon as you feel your physical tension and anger starting to build.

This chapter will describe specific relaxation skills that have been shown to help people who have anger problems. Much of the research backing up these skills has been conducted by psychologist Jerry Deffenbacher and his colleagues at Colorado State University. They have demonstrated that relaxation skills can lead to significant anger reduction. A review of these studies can be found in Howard Kassinove's *Anger Disorders: Definition, Diagnosis, and Treatment*.

PROGRESSIVE MUSCLE RELAXATION

Progressive muscle relaxation (PMR) shows you how to tense and release different groups of your muscles in a specific order. When tensing a muscle group, you focus your attention on the discomfort that you are creating. After about ten seconds, you release, let your muscles relax, and then focus on the heavy, warm feelings you have created. You experience a distinct contrast between your tensing and relaxing.

Learning to recognize the difference between your feelings of tension and relaxation shows you how your anger can build slowly. Your tension can serve as a warning that it is time for you to try to calm yourself before your anger fully gets going.

Before you use PMR, take several precautions. First, if you have any kind of existing muscle problem, consult with your physician. Second, during the tension part of the exercise see that you feel discomfort and not pain. Do not tighten your muscles too vigorously. If you do feel pain in certain muscles, it is best to avoid tensing that muscle group and just focus on the relaxing part of PMR.

The initial PMR procedures take about twenty-five minutes. You tense and release one muscle group at a time, starting with your arm muscles and then moving to your legs, stomach, chest, shoulders, neck and face, until you make your whole body feel calm and relaxed. You can use PMR by following the instructions outlined below. We recommend that you tape-record these instructions so you don't have to interrupt your relaxing by having to look at this book. Afterward, you can follow the instructions by playing the tape back to yourself. You can also purchase an already made audiotape directly from the Albert Ellis Institute for Rational Emotive Behavior Therapy, 45 East 65th Street, New York, NY 10021-6593, by calling 800-323-4738.

Try to tense only one specific muscle group during the tension part of the exercise, while leaving the other parts of your body relaxed. Of course, some overlap will occur. Try to keep your focus on each separate muscle group. It is very normal for other than relaxing thoughts to pop into your mind during the procedure; however, try to gently bring your focus back to the sensations in your muscles. Also make sure you stay awake during the procedure. As pleasant as it may be to drift off to sleep while relaxing, this will not help you learn relaxation skills.

Instructions for PMR

To make your own relaxation tape, don't go too quickly through the following procedure. Allow for the time indicated (in parenthesis) for each exercise. Once your tape is made, you can play it back to yourself in a comfortable and quiet place. You can practice by either sitting up in a comfortable chair or lying down on a bed, couch, or the floor.

START recording here. Gently close your eyes, and sit quietly for a few seconds and focus on smooth breathing (30 seconds).

1. Make fists with both your hands and feel the tension building in your lower arms, hands, and fingers. Focus on that tension and silently describe the uncomfortable pulling sensations to yourself. Hold the tension (10 seconds). Now release the tension and let your hands and arms relax. Focus on the warm, heavy feelings in your hands and notice the contrast with the tension. Focus on your relaxed hands (20 seconds).

2. Bend your arms and take both your elbows and press them firmly into your sides. While pressing your elbows inward, also flex your arm muscles. Notice the tension building up throughout your arms, shoulders, and back. Focus on holding the tension (10 seconds). Now release your arms and let them fall heavily to your sides. Again focus on the heavy, warm, and relaxed feelings in your arms (20 seconds).

3. Moving to your lower legs, flex your feet by trying to point your toes toward your ears. Notice the tension spreading through your feet, ankles, and shins. Hold the tension (10 seconds). Now release the tension in your lower legs. Focus on your sense of comfort as your lower legs become more relaxed (20 seconds).

4. Next, build up the tension in your upper legs by pressing both your knees together and lifting your legs off the bed or chair. Focus on the tension in your thighs and the pulling sensations in your hips. Describe those uncomfortable feelings to yourself (10 seconds). Now release the tension, and let your legs fall heavily onto the bed or chair. Focus on letting go of all the tension in your legs (20 seconds).

5. Next, pull your stomach in toward your spine. Notice the tension in your stomach (10 seconds). Now let your stomach go and relax. Focus on the warmth and relaxation in that part of your body (20 seconds).

6. Next, take in a deep breath and hold it (10 seconds). Notice the tension in your expanded chest. Slowly let the air out and feel the tension disappear. Focus on smooth and normal breathing (20 seconds).

7. Now imagine that your shoulders are on strings and are being pulled up toward your ears. Feel the tension building in your shoulders, your upper back, and neck. Hold that tension (10 seconds). Now just let the tension go and allow your shoulders to droop down. Let them droop down as far as they can go. Notice the difference between the feelings of tension and relaxation (20 seconds).

8. Take your chin and pull it down and try to touch your chest. Notice the pulling and tension in the back of your neck (10 seconds). Now relax, letting go of the tension in your neck. Focus on letting your neck muscles relax (20 seconds).

9. Clench your teeth together and focus on the tension in your jaw. Feel the tight pulling sensation (10 seconds). Then release, letting your mouth drop open and the muscles around your face and jaw relax (20 seconds).

10. Build up the tension in your forehead by forcing yourself to frown, pulling your eyebrows down toward the center. Focus on the tension in your forehead (10 seconds). Now release and try to smooth out all the wrinkles and let your forehead relax (20 seconds).

11. At this point your whole body is probably feeling relaxed and heavy. Every time you breathe out silently say the word "relax" to yourself and imagine that you are breathing out all the tension in your body (do this for 10 breaths).

12. Now bring your attention back to your feet and focus on the warm, heavy feelings (30 seconds). Allow the warm and heavy feelings to slowly travel through your feet and radiate up into your lower legs. Let them linger and circulate there (30 seconds). Allow them to flow into your upper legs as you feel your thighs getting

warmer and heavier (30 seconds). Let the warmth spread from your thighs up into your stomach. Let the warmth settle there (30 seconds). Notice it spread through your back (30 seconds), and then radiate into your chest (30 seconds). Focus on allowing your upper body to become warm, heavy, and relaxed (45 seconds). Next allow the warmth to spread down into your arms (30 seconds), then to your hands (30 seconds). Stay focused on creating that feeling. Once your arms and hands feel warm and heavy, allow the warmth to travel up into your shoulders (30 seconds) and neck (30 seconds). Lastly, let the feelings spread throughout your face and head (30 seconds).

STOP the recording here. As you do this relaxation procedure think about what you are feeling. Try to focus on what it feels like to be relaxed. It is important to be able to remember what relaxation feels like in the different parts of your body. Do not be discouraged if you are not feeling very relaxed after the first try. It may take a few repetitions to get the desired effect. For best results, practice this procedure at least once a day for the next two weeks before moving on to the next set of skills.

Shortening the Relaxation

If you have practiced the above procedure for the last two weeks and are able to achieve a feeling of relaxation, you are ready for the next step. Again find a comfortable, quiet place to sit or lie down. Gently close your eyes and breathe slowly and smoothly. As you exhale, silently repeat the word "relax" to yourself and imagine that you are letting out all of the tension and frustration in your body.

In this shortened version, you will skip the muscle tensing and releasing. Basically, you will be repeating only those procedures from No. 12 in the previous instructions. Starting with your feet, mentally go through each part of your body, imagining it becoming warm, heavy, and relaxed. Try to recall from your previous practice how each part of your body felt when it was relaxed and bring up those feelings. For example, when you think about your shoulders, let them droop as you experience and remember the feelings of relaxation. Again spend enough time on each body area until it feels warm and relaxed, then allow those feelings to spread to the next area. Slowly go through the entire body. Remember, keep your breathing slow and regular.

With repetition you will eventually be able to call up the feelings of relaxation. Practice this method once a day for the next two weeks before moving on to the next set of skills.

PRACTICING RELAXATION SKILLS UNDER FIRE

With practice, by just focusing on bringing up your relaxed feelings you will be able to relax the different areas of your body. In order for these relaxation skills to be really valuable to you, you can learn how to relax yourself under difficult circumstances. To do this, you will create several imagery scenes that can be used as a backdrop for your practice.

Imagery is a technique that psychologists use to help their clients practice different types of skills. In order to use it, you will first create two scenes that usually lead you to feel angry and then practice mentally running them through your mind. After you make yourself angry by imagining these scenes, you will then attempt to use your new relaxation skills to lessen your anger. To prepare the anger scenes, think of yourself as writing a mini–movie script. Each scene should be about a page long and will outline the events of situations where you frequently make yourself angry. As you write the scenes include all the important details such as sights, sounds, smells, what people said, and how you were feeling. The first scene can be about a real-life experience that is associated with a moderate level of anger. The second scene can be about a real-life situation that would usually involve your feeling a very intense level of anger.

Here is what Fran, an advertising executive, wrote for her first scene:

> It's a normal day and I'm driving to work. I arrive about five minutes late and my boss (MariAnne) calls me into her office. Her office is large and covered with gray carpeting. The walls

are painted white with several pictures of sailboats. She is wearing her usual black business suit and has a serious expression on her face. Since she became my supervisor a year ago, MariAnne and I have never really gotten along that well. She always seems to be looking for reasons to dismantle my department. Our budget has been reduced and I have been forced to let go of some good workers. I still feel very angry toward her about that. In addition, she complains that we do not get out enough quality work, which seems especially unfair since our resources have been reduced.

Anyway, MariAnne asks me to sit down on the other side of her large wooden desk. She proceeds to announce that my department is being phased out from running one of our large accounts. Immediately, I start to feel the tension building in my shoulders and a little bit of nausea in my stomach. I try very hard to hold my anger in but I very much want to tell her off. I think to myself that this is extremely unfair and that she is really out to get me. My thoughts also race to the possibility that she and the other managers may be planning to downsize the company and that I will eventually be asked to leave. How will I pay my bills? What about my kids? I want to scream but just sit there and listen and fume silently to myself.

The second scene can involve a very high level of difficulty. Try to base it on a real-life event but feel free to exaggerate it to the worst case you can imagine. Myles has had difficulties with anger control while driving. Here is how he did his second anger scene:

I am on my way home from work one night and it is very hot. The sun is just going down and I can feel my shirt sticking to my body. As I am driving along I can see the traffic slowing up ahead due to some kind of road construction. As I'm waiting to clear the construction area I notice out of the corner of my eye this guy driving along the shoulder of the road where it is illegal to drive, pulling ahead of everybody else. I feel my muscles start to get tight and I say to myself, "This isn't fair!" All of a sudden this guy tries to cut in front of me. I ignore him and keep driving straight. He honks his horn and starts to scream at me. I ignore him some more and think to myself, "This guy is the one behaving like an asshole. Not me!" All of a sudden he leans his head out his car window and spits on my car. Then he tells me to pull over so he can kick my butt. I feel my body start to shake and tremble, I start to yell back, and consider stopping my car to teach this guy a lesson.

Once you have written your anger scenes, you may find it helpful to put them on audiotape so you can play them back at a later time when you are practicing reducing your anger. To begin to use the scenes, first find a quiet location and use the relaxation procedures you have been preferably practicing over the past two weeks. Once you are feeling relaxed, go through the first anger scene by imagining it step by step. You can use the tape recording to help. As you go through the scene, imagine that you are actually experiencing the situation that you have created. Don't just observe it like a movie but really try to feel as if you are participating in it. Allow your anger and tension to build as you imagine the situation unfolding. Tune into your own bodily signs of anger, such as your heart rate, breathing, tension in different parts of your body, thoughts, etc.

Once the scene is done, and you have created some anger and tension in your body, practice once again calling up your feelings of relaxation. Focusing on each muscle group, allow the warm, heavy feelings of relaxation to permeate your entire body.

After you have reduced your tension and are feeling more relaxed, go back to imagining the first anger scene once again. Allow your anger to build, as you did the first time, while imagining the situation unfolding. Once the scene is through, go back and repeat the relaxation procedure until you are once again relaxed and calm. You want to alternate between the relaxation procedure and the anger scene about three times during each practice session. Your practice session will look something like this: (1) begin with relaxation followed by the anger scene and then return to the relaxation, (2) anger scene again followed by relaxation, and (3) anger scene once more followed by relaxation. Always start and end with relaxation.

After a couple of days of practice with the first anger scene, you will get to the point where it becomes difficult to feel any anger when imagining this scene. When this happens it is time to begin practicing with the second anger scene. Follow the same procedures as you did with the first.

There are several benefits to using this method. First, you will be strengthening your relaxation skills in response to difficult situations. You will learn how to calm yourself down physically once your anger starts to build. Second, by repeatedly facing your anger scenes in imagery, you will eventually get used to them. Over time, your physical reaction to those situations will lessen and you will be less likely to overreact should they occur in real life.

Of course, feel free to create other scenes of situations where you make yourself angry that would be useful for you to practice. Whenever a new difficult situation arises, create a scene and go back to practicing your relaxation skills in response to it. Through this method you can learn to relax your body in response to many situations where you typically make yourself angry.

ADDING RATIONAL COPING STATEMENTS

Another tool that can be used while practicing the anger scenes is to rehearse rational coping statements. These are statements designed to help you fight against your angry philosophies and to focus on more rational and constructive ideas. Coping statements can be derived from information already presented in the earlier chapters of this book.

For example, immediately following one of your anger scenes, try rehearsing several rational statements before going through the relaxation procedure. Here are some examples of coping statements that Fran used in response to her imagery scene:

"It is *unpleasant* to be dealt with this way but it is not *horrible*. While I'm still working for this firm I can begin to look for another position."

"Unfairness is part of life. I *can stand* dealing with it and not reacting with anger."

"Even though she is treating me this way, she may have pressures from her supervisors of which I am unaware. I will not help myself in this situation if I take this personally."

Myles created the following rational coping statements to use both when he is practicing his scene and while actually driving:

"I would *prefer* it if all people all the time were considerate when they drove, but that is not the case. Inconsiderate drivers often exist."

"I *can stand* dealing with other people's rudeness, and I do not have to react with anger. In fact, my anger tends to make these annoying situations even worse."

"It is not *awful* if other people cut in front of me while I'm driving. I *can deal* with it."

"Even though other people do sometimes act inconsiderately while driving, they are probably good people in other ways and are just trying to get somewhere in a hurry."

After coming up with your own rational coping statements, go back and rehearse them in response to your anger scenes before focusing on relaxing your body.

USING YOUR SKILLS IN ANGER-AROUSING SITUATIONS

If you have practiced the anger-reducing skills in this chapter, you are now ready to start applying them to real-life situations. First, start to use your body tension as a warning signal that it is time to start putting your new strategies into action. Do not wait until your anger is full-blown. Once you let your anger get to a high level you will find it difficult to use the skills we describe. They work best in the early phases of making yourself angry.

Once you begin to catch yourself becoming angry, repeat some of the rational coping statements you have designed for difficult situations. You may write them on cards, commit them to memory, or play them on a cassette. Have them available when things get tough.

You can next shift into slow, smooth breathing. Again, silently say the word "relax" to yourself as you breathe out. With each breath you exhale, imagine that you are breathing out the tension in your body. Next, try to focus on a specific area of your body and remember the warm, heavy feelings of relaxation. Try to call up those feelings as you breathe and let them spread throughout your body.

As with most of the skills presented in this book, if you consistently practice using them in real-life situations, they will begin to become automatic. Setbacks may of course occur from time to time. When this happens do not get too discouraged but try to go back to practicing your skills. You can always create new anger scenes to help you practice dealing with difficult situations that may come up. Try these procedures whenever you start to feel yourself becoming tense and overly frustrated.

12

Still More Ways of Thinking Yourself Out of Your Anger

REBT, A PIONEERING THINKING APPROACH to personality theory and psychotherapy, has very strong and integrated emotive and behavioral aspects. We have thus far only presented one main cognitive procedure for examining and uprooting angry thoughts and feelings. That is D, or Disputing, of Irrational Beliefs (IBs). Although Disputing is complex and includes Debating and Discriminating, it represents only one philosophic approach to anger.

If you really work at Disputing strongly, intensively, and persistently, you may not need other cognitive methods of disclosing and dislodging your IBs. Yet REBT therapists over the years have discovered several other methods to help you examine and reduce your self-defeating thinking. Let us now describe some important variations on rethinking your anger.

USING THE DISPUTING IRRATIONAL BELIEFS (DIBS) EXERCISE

First, you can use the technique we call Disputing Irrational Beliefs (DIBs), which gives you a more systematic way of taking one of your absolutistic ideas and systematically "ripping it up" many times until you no longer tend to subscribe to it. Like several other REBT methods, you do DIBs occasionally or do it steadily—say, for a few minutes a day for a number of days in a row. I (AE) have outlined the general DIBs technique in the revised edition of *How to Live With a "Neurotic,"* in the final chapter of *A Guide to Rational Living*, and in a separate pamphlet published by the Institute for Rational Emotive Behavior Therapy. Let us present it here as you can specifically apply it to your anger.

Let us suppose, once more, that Jack and Joan promised to share an apartment with you, have persuaded you to go to considerable expense to fix it up, and then have unfairly and irresponsibly backed out of the deal and refused to move in with you or to reimburse you for the trouble and expense you have taken. You feel extremely angry at them and you soon see—in the ABC model of REBT—that your primary IB that creates your anger is, "They *absolutely should not* have treated me that unfairly!"

You now use DIBs to question and challenge this thought. In using DIBs, you ask yourself the following questions, and preferably write down each question on a sheet of paper and also write down your answers, so that you can review and add to them.

Question 1: *What IB do I want to Dispute and surrender?*
Illustrative answer: "They *absolutely should not* have treated me that unfairly!"

Question 2: *Can I rationally support this belief?*
Illustrative answer: "No, I don't think that I can."

Question 3: *What evidence exists of the inaccuracy of this belief?*
Illustrative answers:
1. "Perhaps they didn't even act that unfairly to me. True, I see their action as completely wrong and irresponsible. But they may have, and others may have, a different view of this matter. And their view may have some validity. So I don't even know that I can be 100 percent certain of their wrongness and irresponsibility."
2. "Assuming that I can prove by normal moral standards that they did behave wrongly and unfairly to me, what law of the universe says that they *should* or *must* not behave that way—that they *have* to act fairly? None! Although I and other people see it as

right and proper for them to act fairly to me, they definitely don't *have to* do so."

3. "If they *should have* or *must have* treated me fairly instead of unfairly, they *would* have done so, for how could they avoid doing what they *must* do? The fact that they *didn't* treat me fairly seems to prove conclusively that there is no reason why they *must have* done so."

4. "When I tell myself, 'They should not have treated me that unfairly!' I really seem to mean that (a) the conditions that existed at the time they treated me that way should not have existed and (b) they should not have followed them if they did exist. But of course the conditions of their lives, their history, their personality, their biological makeup, etc., did exist at the time they treated me unfairly. And if these conditions did exist, how could they *not* have gone along with them, as I demand? Suppose, let us say, their parents strongly objected to the very thing that I wanted them to do and suppose that they, because of their undue attachment to these parents, went along with their objections and decided to cop out of our arrangement. By my statement 'They *should not* have treated me that unfairly!' I actually insist that their parents must not have their objections and/or that they should not go along with them. But how can I legitimately *make* their parents give up their objections or *make* them ignore their parents? Naturally, I can't!"

5. "By demanding that they not treat me unfairly, I actually seem to believe the statement, 'Because they theoretically could have *not* acted in that unfair manner, they actually *should not* have acted that way!' But this statement clearly is a non sequitur: its conclusion doesn't logically follow from its premise. No matter how true it may seem that they theoretically could have chosen not to have treated me unfairly, that never means that they therefore actually *must* choose to act fairly."

6. "In demanding that they treat me fairly, I really devoutly believe the proposition, 'Because I strongly want them to act that way, they *have* to give me what I want!' But how valid does that proposition appear? Clearly invalid!"

7. "I also seem to believe that because I have treated them quite fairly throughout our dealings, they *should* and *must* treat me with equal fairness! Another nutty idea!"

8. "I see them as *bad people* for treating me badly. But even if I can prove to virtually everyone's satisfaction that they did treat me unfairly and shabbily, I inaccurately overgeneralize when I label *them*, their entire *personhood*, as bad for treating me in this vile manner. They almost certainly have some good traits too. How, therefore, can I legitimately define *them* as no good?"

9. "When I say, 'They *should not* have treated me that unfairly!' I hypothesize, by using this *should*, an absolutistic *must*. I don't say, 'They *preferably* should treat me fairly,' or 'They *most probably* would get better results for themselves and society if they treated me and others fairly.' I dogmatize and absolutize that 'They *must* treat me fairly!' But as far as I know, I can prove no absolutes, and inventing them and feeling completely convinced of their truth is futile."

10. "While I cannot prove the truth of my belief, 'They should not have treated me that unfairly,' I *can* prove that if I continue to subscribe to this belief, I will in all probability feel very angry at them and continue to feel enraged for perhaps months or years to come, thus interfering with my chances of dealing with them effectively. Although my anger-creating statements seem unprovable, the evil results of my devoutly believing them appear eminently provable! Therefore, I had better give them up!"

11. "By demanding that they must treat me fairly, I imply that I *can't stand* their unfair treatment of me and that I can only survive and lead a happy existence if some force in the universe makes them correct their erroneous ways and begin to treat me fairly. Obviously, my ideas in this respect are hokum. For although I'll never *like* their unfair treatment, I *can* certainly stand it and, if I stop foolishly making myself enraged at them, I can have a long and reasonably happy life in spite of their past, present, and future unfairness."

Question 4: *Does any evidence exist of the accuracy of my belief about Jack and Joan—of my assumption that they should not have treated me unfairly and that they are bad people for doing what they should not have done?*

Illustrative answer: "No, no good evidence that I can think of. I can obtain some data showing that they treated me unfairly, by probably getting a consensus from many other people that they did so. I can therefore contend that their *behavior* is bad or immoral. But I don't have any evidence whatever that they are *bad people* because of that behavior. So, at most, my belief about them is only partially accurate—and significant aspects of it appear highly exaggerated and essentially inaccurate."

Question 5: *What bad things can actually happen to me if Joan and Jack continue to treat me unfairly?*

Illustrative answers:

1. "I will not be reimbursed for the time, trouble, and money I have spent in fixing up the apartment they agreed to share with me and will therefore continue to suffer real inconvenience as a result of their withdrawing from our agreement."

2. "They may possibly give people a false impression of our differences, and convince them that they acted correctly and that I acted wrongly. This would blacken my name and reputation."

3. "As a result of their disliking me and perhaps inducing others to dislike me, too, I may suffer more inconveniences."

4. "Living in my new apartment by myself or having to share it with someone else, as a result of their backing out of their agreement with me, may well prove highly annoying."

5. "I may continue to have hassles with them, particularly if we remain in contact in the future. Even if we somehow resolve our differences, we all will tend to have a bad taste in our mouths and will lose our previous degree of trust and friendship."

"All these things will be bad if they occur but they will not be *terrible* and *awful*. I can stand them and still lead a reasonably happy life."

Question 6: *What good things can happen or can I make happen even if Jack and Joan continue to treat me unfairly and I can't stop them from doing so?*

Illustrative answers:

1. "I can gain in assertiveness by confronting them with their unfairness and by trying to get them, even though unsuccessfully, to change their attitude and behavior toward me."

2. "I can actually enjoy living by myself or finding another person to share my new apartment."

3. "The time and energy that I now expend in maintaining a friendship with them I can put toward doing friendly things with others and enjoying myself in other ways."

4. "I can practice my discussing and arguing skills through attempting to get them to see things differently and to change their unfair actions toward me."

5. "I can use this unfair situation with them as a challenge to work on my own attitudes, to acknowledge that I largely create my own rage when others mistreat me, to change my anger-creating philosophy of life, and to prepare myself for more constructive action and less destructive rage and temper tantrums in the future when other people treat me unfairly."

The DIBs exercise simply organizes some of the more important aspects of disputing IBs when obnoxious and unwanted situations arise. It consists of a systematic approach to Disputing through a particular set of questions that you keep using whenever you feel emotionally upset at C. You can apply DIBs, of course, to feelings of anxiety, depression, despair, self-pity, and low frustration tolerance as well as anger. As you may have already noted, this technique encourages a concerted, methodical approach, aims at your using it regularly, and encourages you to do it in writing or with the use of a tape recorder, so that you can keep reviewing your previous Disputing and improve it.

USING REFERENTING OR HIGHLIGHTING
THE COSTS OF SELF-DEFEATING BEHAVIORS

Another cognitive method of uprooting IBs consists of a technique invented by Joseph Danysh (and outlined in his book *Stop Without Quitting*). It uses the principles of general semantics originated by

Alfred Korzybski. Korzybski notes that virtually all humans naturally and easily overgeneralize and often invent misleading meanings. They consequently tend to defeat themselves and behave unhealthily by making inaccurate conclusions resulting from their poor language (semantic) usage. Several of Korzybski's followers, such as Wendell Johnson and S. I. Hayakawa, have applied his teachings to the field of emotional disturbance, and much of their thinking has been incorporated into REBT, which several authorities describe as one of the leading semantic therapies.

As stated, Joseph Danysh's theory embodies these principles of semantic overgeneralization, and in his referenting technique, he provides you with a practical, thinking tool for attending to some of your IBs and gives you a hardheaded method of changing them.

As applied to the problem of anger, you can use the *referenting* technique as follows: Suppose you feel exceptionally angry whenever you hear about someone who has "made you" angry in the past and suppose you now want to reduce your irate feelings. Telling yourself, "Don't feel angry. Don't feel angry," won't really work. If anything, you may succeed only in suppressing your anger. You will not undo it.

Your emotional problem here probably consists of your *poor referenting*—of confusing your ideas about the person's *behavior* with your ideas about the *person himself*—in a sloppy, bigoted, and overgeneralized manner. Thus, if someone else asks you to give the meanings or associations that immediately pop into your head when you think of the person's behavior, you will probably say something like, "His behavior is no good, rotten, unfair, horrible, and evil. He is a no-good individual, a rotten person who is always unfair. He is someone whom I particularly cannot tolerate."

This type of exclusive, one-sided, and overgeneralized merging of the terms describing a person's behavior with the person himself probably will cause you to feel exceptionally hostile toward him. As long as you insist on making this connection, you will find it almost impossible to reduce your angry feelings and view your opponent's behavior in a more accurate light.

Danysh's technique of referenting forces you to go beyond your prejudiced one-sidedness about people's behavior and to use several better terms to describe both people and their actions. Referenting consists of taking a relatively vague word, such as "behavior," and forcing yourself to list the much more specific referents, or concrete descriptions, that comprise it. Danysh's method particularly encourages you to bring to your own attention *many* of the diverse meanings of a term, instead of a few limited (and prejudiced) meanings.

For example, while thinking specifically of someone's—say, a friend's—poor behavior, write a list of negative terms to describe that behavior, such as "rotten, no good, unfair, horrible, awful, evil, and lousy." Then, on the same sheet, go out of your way to think of and write down any terms which you might think of to describe the positive and good aspects of her behavior—such as "fair most of the time if not this time, probably fair from her own point of view if not mine, acts in her own self-interest as do I, forthright, determined, assertive, sometimes very nice and considerate of other people, concerned with other people in general." Finally, you can write down some of the aspects of her behavior that are neutral—things she does or says that are not "good" or "bad" but just parts of her makeup, such as "interested in many aspects of life, highly absorbed in music, not devoted to sports, makes many public presentations."

By referenting, as accurately and completely as you can, *all* your different ideas about this friend's behavior, you force yourself to keep in mind a more holistic, more accurate, and less one-sided view of her in general. Thus, your one-sided view about her behavior—"rotten, no good, unfair, horrible"—will tend to diminish. You will begin to see it pluralistically and not as you might tend to fictionalize and label it in your mind because of a *particular* instance of bad behavior.

If you force yourself to use this referenting technique, especially when you feel very angry toward someone, you will find that you can de-emphasize her bad traits and thus start to acquire a much more enlightened, accurate, and realistic view of that person. Referenting won't make you automatically forgiving and unangry with all people whom you encounter and accepting of the nasty actions they perform against you. But it frequently will help. When you get into the habit of doing it, you will tend to find after a while that you stop making yourself as often and as intensely angry as you now feel.

USING PARADOXICAL INTENTION

Another good method which you can use both cognitively and behaviorally consists of what Viktor Frankl calls paradoxical intention. Various other therapists use it in different ways and often call it different names. In REBT, we sometimes refer to it as reducing irrational beliefs to absurdity. Using paradoxical intention, you can take any idea and reduce or enlarge it to absurdity by exaggerating in your mind the wildest implications of the original idea. For instance, if you want someone to do something for you and you make yourself angry because he refuses to cooperate, exaggerate your wish for power and control over him:

"Of course he has to do what I want him to do! I have absolute control over his behavior. If he tells me that he will jump through hoops to please me and then refuses to go through with this jumping, I can easily put him in chains and whip him until he jumps and jumps and jumps! In fact, if I want him to give me a million dollars or to grovel in the dust before me ten times a day, he has no choice but to do my bidding! Because I desire him to do anything whatever, he completely has to do it! And if he refuses, I can immediately send down thunderbolts and annihilate him."

If you take the idea of having control over a person to a ridiculous extreme such as this, you will soon see that you really have virtually no control over him and that he has a right to do whatever he wishes even when he unfairly inconveniences you by exercising that right. You will see that human nature does not exist as you command it to exist. You will then give up your own foolish expectation that people will always behave as you desire.

Just as you can use paradoxical intention in your mind as described above, you can also practice it behaviorally. If people treat you unfairly and you feel exceptionally angry, instead of planning to punish them, you can deliberately force yourself to take the opposite track and to act very nicely to them. You can, for example, keep befriending them in various ways: invite them to interesting functions that you know they will enjoy; do them special favors; show unusual consideration and kindness toward them. By such paradoxical behavior, you will first of all practice feeling unangry instead of angry. Second, you will, by turning the other cheek in this manner, set them a good example and show them that their unfair treatment doesn't necessarily have to produce rage in another person. Third, you may encourage them to look again at their behavior and to see how badly they treated you. Finally, you may inspire them to act nicely toward you and even make reparations for the wrongs they have already done you.

We do not contend that this kind of turning-the-other-cheek philosophy will always work or is invariably wise. But if you use it judiciously and realize that you do it for paradoxical reasons (and not necessarily in every instance where someone treats you unfairly), you may gain considerably by it and help reduce your feelings of rage.

Paradoxical intention also may reduce human stubbornness. If people treat you unfairly and you even recognize that they have an emotional problem, you may still *perversely* continue to feel and act angrily toward them in order to maintain your false integrity—to make yourself feel "stronger" when, in actuality, you keep acting weakly. This paradox may occur between you and your parents, for instance, during your childhood. They advise you, mainly for your own good, to get up promptly when the alarm clock rings in the morning and to get yourself off in time for school. You don't like to get up that early, and you lazily (with your low frustration tolerance!) resist. But you also see that by resisting, you keep getting into trouble with the school authorities and sabotaging some of your own goals—for example, to get good marks in high school and therefore to get into a good college of your own choice.

Perversely, you may tell yourself something like, "I won't get up early to please my parents! Darned if I will! That would prove me a ninny who only goes along for their ride. I'll show them! I'll deliberately stay in bed late and prove my strength and follow my own integrity!" If you act that way as a child—or, for that matter, as an adult—you merely fool yourself. Because your parents advise you to get up early, you foolishly—and perversely—convince yourself that if you do so, you will follow their rules and do it for *them*. You consider that kind of rule-following a weakness, when actually it would be a strength. You "strongly" resist them and actually act foolishly—weakly—when you do.

Similarly, often, with anger. You may feel furious about unfair treatment and see your fury as self-defeating and perhaps as encouraging others to treat you even more unfairly. Yet instead of trying to change your commanding philosophy about people's behavior, you may cling to that philosophy and convince yourself that you strongly and rationally feel enraged and that you'd *better* angrily show offenders their faults. By convincing yourself that to do otherwise would make you "weak" and lose your own integrity, you choose to persist with your rage even though you partly realize that it is irrational. Actually, to give up your anger while continuing to strongly dislike people's unfair acts would make you much stronger and get you better results. But if you see it differently, and perhaps deliberately make yourself even more enraged and vindictively go after the person who has wronged you, you will continue to feel angry.

When you interrupt "strong" perversity with paradoxical intention and deliberately get yourself to think nicely about and act kindly toward others in spite of their unfairness, you paradoxically fight your own irrationality and tend to give it up. In terms of what you really want for yourself and the good relationships you desire, you can get better results by acting in this paradoxical manner.

Rachel Hare outlines another form of paradoxical intention which I (AE) have used to help my clients cut down their angry feelings and actions. It consists of giving yourself limiting conditions under which you can allow yourself to have temper tantrums. One of my clients felt exceptionally irate and combative every time he thought that someone on the street spit in his direction and spewed some spit on him. I persuaded him to contract with himself that he would only let himself get angry when he could prove, with clear-cut observational evidence, preferably with the confirmation of other observers, that some spit had actually landed on him. Since he could rarely prove this, his fits of anger subsided greatly.

To use the same paradoxical technique on yourself, pick a set of conditions where you feel you have been treated unfairly and where you frequently feel and act with rage. Deliberately limit this set of conditions. Contract to allow yourself to get angry, for example, only when (1) everyone agrees that people have truly treated you unfairly, (2) everyone also agrees that the unfairness has caused you a considerable amount of harm, and (3) you can prove to yourself that you have lost a considerable sum of money by the unfair treatment.

If you allow yourself, in this paradoxical manner, freely to feel and express your rage while also deliberately restricting yourself, you may soon see that you can live with your own restrictions, that you actually create your anger yourself, and that you have the power to limit and control it. Such paradoxical techniques work because they stop you from thinking, desperately, "I must feel angry" or "I must not feel angry." They give you a wider range of possible reactions and help you convince yourself that you can function in this wider range.

THE USE OF HUMOR

Humor dramatically interrupts your overly serious manner of looking at certain unpleasant events and thereby needlessly making yourself angry. Jerry Deffenbacher, a leading researcher in treating anger, recommends the use of silly humor to reduce rage. As he notes, making fun of your own flying off the handle helps you step back and rethink some of your rigidly held rage-creating Beliefs.

REBT therapists frequently use various types of jocularity to help their clients poke fun at their own solemnity and, both cognitively and emotively, learn to accept themselves better. I (AE) gave a now somewhat famous paper, "Fun as Psychotherapy," at the annual convention of the American Psychological Association in Washington, D.C., in 1976, and made a great hit because I sang—yes, sang—two of my rational humorous songs in the course of my presentation.

I pointed out in this paper:

If human disturbance largely consists of overseriousness and if, as in Rational Emotive Behavior Therapy, therapists had better make a hard-headed attack on some of their clients' silly thinking, what better vehicle for doing this kind of Disputing than humor and fun?...Let me briefly mention that my therapeutic brand of humor consists of practically every kind of drollery ever invented—such as taking things to extreme, reducing ideas to absurdity, paradoxical intentions, puns, witticisms, irony, whimsy, evocative language, slang, deliberate use of sprightly off-color language, and various other kinds of jocularity.

Following this REBT lead, you can frequently laugh at yourself when you see yourself getting angry, look for the gross exaggeration in your ideas about what others *must* do to satisfy you and how things *should* go right to make your life easier, and thereby cognitively and emotively attack such silly notions. When you demand good behavior in others, you can remind yourself, "Oh, yes, I always act perfectly well myself. I *never* treat people unfairly or go back on my promises to them. Well, hardly ever!" When you think that you absolutely need others' approval and that they are complete vermin for not giving it to you, remind yourself what a love slob or commander of the world you have made yourself into. When you whine and scream because poor economic, political, or social conditions exist, tell yourself something like: "Oh, yes, I run the universe, and whatever I want has to, in fact *immediately* has to, come about. Everyone else has to live with frustration and annoyance, but not *me!*"

Call to your mind, also, what we often tell our REBT clients: "Life, whether we like it or not, generally is spelled H-A-S-S-L-E. Tough taffy!" When you demand that you must have certainty and that you can't stand it when you don't have guarantees of success, love, fairness, and ease, tell yourself, "I think I'll engrave a beautiful certificate which absolutely, with no shadow of a doubt, guarantees that I will always get exactly what I want at the very second that I want it. Then I'll get along wonderfully well and won't have to feel angry about anything!"

Keep using humor, directed against your nutty ideas but not, of course, against yourself as a person. And if you want to sing to yourself (or others) some of REBT's rational humorous songs, you can use these from the songbook *A Garland of Rational Songs:**

WHINE, WHINE, WHINE!
(to the tune of the Yale "Whiffenpoof Song")

I cannot have all my wishes filled—,
  Whine, whine, whine!
I cannot have every frustration stilled—
  Whine, whine, whine!
Life really owes me the things that I miss,
Fate has to grant me eternal bliss!
And if I must settle for less than this—
  Whine, whine, whine!

PERFECT RATIONALITY
(to the tune of Luigi Denza's "Funiculì, Funiculà")

Some think the world must have a right direction—
  And so do I, and so do I!
Some think that, with the slightest imperfection,
  They can't get by—and so do I!
For I, I have to prove I'm superhuman,
  And better far than people are!—
To show I have miraculous acumen—
  And always rate among the Great!—

---

*Lyrics by Albert Ellis. Copyright by Albert Ellis Institute for Rational Emotive Behavior Therapy.

Perfect, perfect rationality
Is, of course, the only thing for me!
How can I ever think of being
   If I must live fallibly?
Rationality must be a perfect thing for me!

I WISH I WERE NOT CRAZY
(to the tune of Dan Emmet's "Dixie Land")

Oh, I wish I were really put together—
Smooth and fine as patent leather!
   Oh, how great to be mated
   To this lovely state!
But I'm afraid that I was fated
To be rather aberrated—
   Oh, how sad to be mad
   As my mom and my dad!
Oh, I wish I were not crazy! Hooray, hooray!
I wish my mind were less inclined
To be the kind that's hazy!
I could, of course, decide to be less crazy;
But I, alas, am just too blasted lazy!

LOVE ME, LOVE ME, ONLY ME!
(to the tune of "Yankee Doodle")

Love me, love me, only me,
   Or I'll die without you!
Make your love a guarantee,
   So I can never doubt you!
Love me, love me totally,
   And I shall get by, dear;
But if I must rely on me,
   I'll hate you till I die, dear!

Love me, love me all the time,
   Thoroughly and wholly;
Life turns into slush and slime,

'Less you love me solely.
Love me with great tenderness,
With no ifs and buts, dear;
For if you love me somewhat less
I'll hate your rotten guts dear!

REDUCING ANGER IN CLOSE RELATIONSHIPS

Since we have done marriage and family counseling for many years, people frequently ask us how they can check or control their anger at their spouses or at others with whom they have a close relationship. Well they might! A famous marriage counselor, Dr. David Mace, pointed out in a valuable article in the *Journal of Marriage and Family Counseling* that conscious and unconscious feelings of anger probably interfere with love and disrupt more intimate ties than do any other causes. Dr. Mace rightly takes to task the "marital fighting" concepts of George Bach and his followers and points out that if you tend to argue and fight with your mate, you can use the REBT approach of dissolving and dissipating your anger rather than that of expressing it or diverting it.

More concretely, he outlines three main methods of doing this:

1. Acknowledge your anger. Tell your partner, "I feel angry at you," just as you would say, "I feel tired," or "I feel frightened."

2. Renounce your anger as unhealthy. Even though your mate has treated you badly or unfairly, face the fact that you largely create your own anger, that you need not do so, and that you usually harm your relationship by feeling it and by expressing it against your partner.

3. Ask your partner for help. Show him or her that you have a problem in dealing with your anger, and see if he or she can suggest some plans to help rid you of it and to make your relationship better.

We highly endorse the above suggestions of Mace's. In a follow-up article to Mace's, also published in the *Journal of Marriage and Family Counseling*, I (AE) add these additional REBT methods to help you deal with your anger at anyone with whom you have a marital or other close relationship:

4. Acknowledge your anger to yourself. Don't merely inform your mate about your angry feelings, but frankly tell yourself, "Look: Let me face it. I really feel angry at my partner. Not merely displeased; not merely annoyed at his/her *behavior*. I feel angry at my mate as a person. I feel condemning, demanding about *him or her*." Unless you do something like this, you will not feel in touch with your anger and will "acknowledge" it only through weak lip-service. Once you acknowledge your ire to *yourself* and work at defusing it, you may then choose (or not choose) to express it to your mate—depending on his or her vulnerability, and on other special considerations.

5. Assume full responsibility for your anger. Do not hesitate to admit that you created it, that you angered yourself. Say to yourself something like: "Yes, my mate may have acted badly and treated me unfairly, but he/she only frustrated me, gave me what I didn't want. I made myself feel annoyed and irritated about his/her poor behavior, which are healthy negative feelings—because I do honestly want him/her to act differently and feel sorry when he/she doesn't. But I also, quite unhealthily, *made myself* angry by commanding and whining that he/she *must not* act that way; *has to do* what I want; renders my whole life terrible and awful when he or she doesn't; and consequently is a thoroughly rotten *person. I* chose to think this way and thereby enraged myself at my partner. And I can, if I want to do so, choose to think differently and change my feelings of anger into healthier feelings of disappointment, sorrow, and annoyance." If you fully, in this manner, acknowledge your own responsibility for making yourself angry, you will by that very admission tend to rid yourself of a good part of your angry feelings.

6. Accept yourself *with* your anger. As soon as you condemn or damn yourself for having neurotic symptoms—anger, anxiety, depression, feelings of worthlessness, or anything else—you tend to interfere with ridding yourself of such symptoms. For if you see yourself as a *worm* for feeling, let us say, enraged at your mate, how

can a total worm like you act unwormily? And while you keep berating yourself for stupidly making yourself angry, how can you have the time and energy to understand exactly what you told yourself to create your anger and to work at minimizing it?

Accept yourself, then, *with* your anger. This does not mean, as some psychological writings imply, that you had better view angry feelings as good, healthy, or constructive. You can see them as normal in the sense that they are part of the human condition—an aspect of your human fallibility. But they still, almost always, defeat you—and, as David Mace points out, tend to harm your intimate relationships.

7. *Stop making yourself anxious, depressed, and self-blaming.* As you learn to accept yourself, no matter how enraged you feel or how foolishly you act when angry, you can also learn to accept yourself with any of your other "wrong" or "bad" behaviors. If you do this, you will give up much of your vulnerability—the feelings of hurt and self-pity that often help you feel very angry.

8. *Look for the philosophic source of your anger.* After fully acknowledging your feelings of anger, if you do not condemn yourself for having them, you can look for their philosophic sources. Realize (as shown throughout this book) that just about every time you feel enraged, you have a profound assumption behind rage, and that your assumption includes some *should, ought*, or *must*. Consequently, *cherchez le* should, *cherchez le* must! Look for the *should*, look for the *must*!

In anger at your mate, you frequently hold the *must* of resentment—"You *must* treat me kindly, considerately, lovingly, and approvingly!"—and the *must* of low frustration tolerance—"The conditions under which I live *must* turn out nicely and nonfrustratingly so that I easily get practically everything I want without too much effort."

More specifically, when enraged at your mate, you usually tell yourself: (a) "My partner *must* treat me considerately and lovingly. He/she actually behaves unfairly and disapprovingly. I *can't stand* this behavior! I find it *awful!* What a total rotter he/she is!" And (b) "I joined together with this mate in order to experience joy and happiness. But unpleasant conditions in our relationship exist. They *must* not continue to exist in this horrible way! How *terrible* that they do! I *can't bear* it! Mating is an absolutely frightful state, and I hate it, hate it, hate it!"

So look—and keep looking until you find—your own *shoulds*, *oughts*, and *musts* about (a) your mate; (b) your children; (c) the conditions under which you live; (d) your in-laws; (e) your sex relations with your mate, etc. As soon as you zero in on and clearly understand these *musts*, you locate the most important sources of your hatred and rage—as I (AE) and Dr. Robert A. Harper point out in *A Guide to Successful Marriage*.

9. Distinguish your *wishes* about your mate and your relationship from your *musturbatory commands*. You can very legitimately tell yourself, "I would much rather have sex with my mate twice a week than have it once every two weeks." But you can then foolishly add, "And therefore, he/she *must* have it the way I want it!" Just about every one of your absolutistic demands on your partner has a somewhat realistic and reasonable wish or preference behind it. Search in your head and your heart for *both* the wish *and* the command that insists you have to fulfill or satisfy this wish. Separate the two very, very clearly!

10. Dispute and debate your absolutistic *musts*. Your merely *understanding* your demands on your mate (and on the universe) will not solve your problem. For you can easily say to yourself, "Oh, yes, I see now that I feel terribly angry toward my partner because I keep commanding that she/he do exactly what I prefer. Well, maybe I'd better give up those commands and translate them back into wishes." Fine—but not enough!

Unless you very actively, persistently, and strongly Dispute, question, and challenge those demands, you probably will never give them up. Only by making a thorough change in your philosophic assumptions, your absolutistic *shoulds*, will you probably reduce your angry feelings. And by reduce, we do not mean suppress, repress, avoid, or sweep under the rug. We mean change them to healthy negative emotions instead of unproductive rage.

11. Employ behavioral and emotive means of undermining your

feelings of anger. As noted throughout this book, and especially in chapters 9 and 10, you not only create or manufacture your own angry feelings but then reinforce them by various emotive and behavioral acts. You therefore had better use forceful, dramatic, and active-directive behavioral methods to reduce your anger. Thus, emotively, you can deliberately act lovingly rather than angrily to your mate. You can train yourself to empathize more effectively with your partner's point of view and feelings. You can practice what Carl Rogers calls unconditional positive regard or what in REBT we call unconditional self-acceptance. You can use non-blaming I-statements instead of condemning you-statements about your mate's behavior. You can express your hostile feelings about your partner to other people (e.g., friends) rather than directly to him/her. You can role-play some of your angry reactions to your mate. You can use Rational Emotive Imagery to let yourself imagine your mate's acting very badly, let yourself feel very angry at him/her, and then practice changing your feelings to disappointment rather than rage.

As for behavioral methods, you can use several to help you reinforce your antimusturbatory attack on feelings of anger. You can deliberately stay in anger-inciting situations or court them to give yourself practice in coping with such conditions and in changing your hostility-creating philosophies as you deal with them. You can practice assertiveness instead of passivity to ward off your building up unnecessary feelings of rage when you do not assert yourself with your mate. You can use operant conditioning or self-management methods and reward yourself when you react unangrily.

You can employ behavior rehearsal methods and train yourself (by working with a model or role-playing partner) to react more healthily when your mate does some presumably upsetting act. You can make written or oral contracts with your mate to do some things that he or she wishes you to do, provided that he or she will do other things that you would prefer. You can use relaxation, meditation, thought stopping, or other desensitizing and distraction methods to take yourself, at least temporarily, out of anger-arousing situations and to give yourself extra time to work against your grandiose commanding philosophies.

In many different ways, then, you can apply the anger-reducing methods outlined in this book to acknowledge your making yourself incensed at your love partner and to reduce your anger and enjoy more of the good feelings that your relationship may bring about.

13

Additional Ways
of Reducing Your Anger

CAN YOU BE COMPLETELY RATIONAL about dealing with your anger and reducing it? Probably not. As we have already shown, you naturally and easily enrage yourself at dangers and Adversities. Your very life sometimes depends upon your doing so. Your underlying resentment and your extreme displeasure with people and things that unfairly afflict you are upsetting feelings that may well plague you. But they also protect you, propel you to change poor conditions, and have other real advantages. Maybe surrendering them entirely will add to your life. But not always!

Is uncontrolled indulgence in your "honest" temper tantrums therefore a good answer to your "overwhelming" frustrations? Not exactly! Why not take a more rational middle-ground position—let yourself feel greatly displeased with oppressive conditions and energetically push yourself to improve them while giving up your whining demands that they *absolutely should not*, *must not* exist and that your life is completely *horrible* if they do? Yes, why not?

More specifically, a rational, practical approach to anger includes several important efforts. Try, especially:

- A hardheaded, persistent acknowledgment that you do feel senselessly enraged rather than sensibly annoyed at obnoxious happenings.
- The full admission that you largely—though not exclusively—

made yourself feel furious and (fortunately!) have the choice of continuing, or not continuing, to feel that way.

- The knowledge that you can distinctly control and reduce your stormy feelings, although you can rarely reduce them to absolute zero.
- The ardent recognition that fury often does you and those you care for considerably more harm than good.
- The solid determination to work—and keep working—to lessen your rage.
- Consistent effort and practice to act on your determination to make yourself distinctly less angry and enraged.

Assuming that you are developing along these lines and are really pushing yourself to follow the many REBT methods that we have been describing in the previous chapters of this book, here are a number of additional ways you can avoid indulging in harmful fits of anger.

REVIEW THE PRACTICAL RESULTS OF ANGER

Albert Bandura's investigations of hostility as well as the reinforcement theories of B.F. Skinner raise three major points: (1) Anger and violence rarely arise from "good" social interactions but generally follow from experiences that include—or that *appear* to include—serious frustrations and deprivations. (2) Once we react in certain hostile ways to frustrations and annoyances, we get reinforced and/or penalized by our reactions. Hostility either encourages us to remove the stimuli that we find obnoxious or it brings us other satisfactions (for example, the pleasure of feeling superior to the people we fight). Or else our rage penalizes us— helps bring on counterattacks from those we hate and attack. (3) After getting reinforced or penalized for our aggressive feelings and moves, we finally can weigh the short-term and long-term advantages and disadvantages of the results we achieve and can reduce frustrating conditions and then decide how we will react to the frustrations that still remain.

For example, let us suppose, once again, that Jack and Joan

promised to share an apartment with you and, after persuading you to go to great expense to fix it up, have refused to move in with you. They have thus set up a set of frustrating conditions for you to deal with. If you then choose to feel and act angrily toward them, you will get certain reinforcements and penalties. On the reinforcing side, you may stop being friendly to them, get some money from them, or feel quite superior to them because you acted "well" and they acted "badly." On the penalizing side, you may encourage them to treat you still worse in the future, be disapproved of by some of your mutual friends for your vindictiveness toward them, and consume valuable time and energy futilely trying to get restitution from them. These reinforcements and penalties will tend, consciously or unconsciously, to make you feel more or less angry when similar frustrations and annoyances occur in your future life.

Finally, after feeling angry at Joan and Jack for a while and perhaps instituting some kind of a feud with them, you (as a human) have the ability to review the entire situation and put it in the context of your general life. You can decide, for example, that your anger has some advantages, but that it can also contribute to health problems like high blood pressure and therefore bring you more harm than good. You can decide that your hostility makes you feel superior to Joan and Jack, but that this kind of an ego game really isn't very rewarding. You can decide that you can live successfully with your displeasure and your anger, but that you could live more happily if you arranged to stay away from people like them in the future and thus could "block" the frustrations that accompany such relationships.

If, in other words, you make yourself fully aware of how frustrations contribute to your anger, of what kinds of rewards and penalties immediately tend to accompany it, and of what long-term consequences may result from your rewarding angry "victories," you begin to understand many of the complex roots of hostility. You then have a wide range of solutions available to you, including changing the frustrating events or Adversities that contribute to your irate feelings; arranging for different kinds of reinforcers and penalties that will tend to make you feel less angry when faced with Adversities; taking a long-range instead of a short-range hedonistic view of the disadvantages of hostility; and changing your outlook toward frustrations so that you make them seem less horrible.

As ancient Greek philosophers noted, knowledge is power. The more you understand the biological, social, cognitive, and other sources of your angry feelings and actions, the greater are your chances of reducing their poor results and of looking for better solutions than those that go with rage.

Although frustration does not seem to directly or invariably cause anger, it certainly significantly contributes to it! Most people who suffer severe deprivation have a strong tendency to upset themselves about this—and often to lash out angrily at frustrating people and conditions. Although you had better work to raise your frustration tolerance, you can also wisely work to reduce your frustrations themselves.

You *don't have* to work at a boring job, stay with annoying friends, let your mate or children keep taking advantage of you, or remain with an unsatisfying sex partner. Temporarily, you may help yourself by deliberately and unangrily remaining in these unpleasant kinds of conditions so as to raise your own low frustration tolerance. Temporarily! But in the long run you almost always have better alternatives. Look for them. Work at arranging them. On the other hand, don't try to live with *zero* frustration (for you won't succeed!). Sometimes don't even strive for minimal frustration (for you may thereby lose out on potential pleasures). But needless restrictions you really don't need. Do something to reduce them, if not immediately, at least ultimately. And, often— soon!

INCREASING FRUSTRATION TOLERANCE

Anger and violence rarely stem from mere frustration but from low frustration tolerance. When you feel furious, you insist that whatever frustrates you *should* and *ought* not to exist—that it not only is unfair, but that this unfairness, *must* not prevail, that you *can't stand* it, and that those who unduly balk and block you are almost total vermin who *should* not act the way they indubitably do.

You can find an antidote to this kind of thinking by teaching yourself higher frustration tolerance. How? By seeing that frustration *should* exist (because it does), as should unfairness and injustice. In this respect, you can heed the words of Erich Fromm:

> First of all, we might consider a basic fact of life: that nothing important is achieved without accepting frustration. The idea that one can learn without effort, i.e., without frustration, may be good as an advertising slogan, but is certainly not true in the acquisition of major skills. Without the capacity to accept frustration man would hardly have developed at all. And does not everyday observation show that many times people suffer frustration without having an aggressive response? What can, and often does, produce aggression is what the frustration *means* to the person.

To add to what Fromm says, you can achieve high frustration tolerance by:

1. Acknowledging your tendency to demand that frustration *must not* exist.
2. Realizing that you will almost always defeat yourself unless you reduce your demandingness.
3. Firmly deciding to give it up and replace it with a desire but not an absolutistic insistence that you be less frustrated.
4. Determinedly working to live up to that decision.

Your philosophy *about* frustration, then, is the real issue, and even when you have little control over being frustrated, you can definitely change that philosophy. Personal growth doesn't stem from avoiding frustration but from facing it and giving up your whining about it.

ATTACKING NARCISSISM AND GRANDIOSITY

As Gregory Rochlin points out, narcissism or childish grandiosity has profound roots in human nature and tends to underlie much of our behavior. We don't merely want others to love and care for us; we utterly insist that they do, and we frequently feel shattered when they don't. Such shattering is self-induced since *we*, rather than *they*, damn ourselves by our dire need for their acceptance. We often foolishly claim that *they* destroy us by rejecting our "needs." This frequently leads to our feeling exceptionally angry and acting violently against those who presumably have failed us. Rochlin emphasizes how hostility often springs from wounded self-esteem. While he sometimes neglects its other important sources, he does have a point: a good deal of our fury against others arises from the "hurt" they give us—the "hurt" to our narcissistic demands for approval.

Moral: You can give up your infantile narcissism if this is one of the main sources of your anger. You don't *have* to run the universe. You don't *need* to feel good about yourself mainly because others acknowledge your outstandingness. No reason exists why you *must* have the center of the stage or why you *should* receive even minimum respect from others.

No, the world *doesn't* care too much for you and most likely never will. The more famous you get, moreover, the more enemies you will tend to make. The better you behave toward some people, the more they may take advantage of you. The universe has no *special* interest in you, nor ever will. Now, how can you fully face and accept that "cruel," "cold" fact and live happily in spite of it? If you can, one of the main sources of your anger against others will be significantly reduced.

As both Freud and Adler noted many years ago and as stated in the earliest writings on REBT, much anger stems from childish grandiosity. As humans, we often believe that because others *can* treat us well, and because we *may* benefit from this kind of treatment, they should bestow it on us. As H. Peters has noted, "There have been philosophers, such as Bertrand Russell, who have held that jealousy is always inappropriate as an emotion, basically because it presupposes unjustifiable claims to a special relationship with another person.

If whenever you feel angry at someone you fully face the fact that you imply a godlike command that this person *ought* to accord you special treatment, and if you firmly rip up that *ought* many times and replace it with "It would be *preferable* if this person treated me specially, but the chances are that he or she often won't," you will minimize your anger.

Watch your grandiosity! Watch your dogmatism! The stronger you feel about a cause, the more you may ignore its limitations. Try to bring these to mind, too. And see if you can determinedly go after what you want—without enraging yourself and insisting that because you find it right and proper, it *absolutely must* prevail.

History, as Daniel J. Boorstin points out, provides us with many striking illustrations of the consequences of rage, ranging from the prolonged wars in ancient Israel and Greece, to Hitler's and Stalin's holocausts, right up to the numerous religious, political, economic, and other bloodbaths still very much with us. Moreover, Boorstin reminds us, history also helps us to uproot our utopianism and respect our possibilities for progress:

> "The voice of the intellect," observed Sigmund Freud (who did not underestimate the role of the irrational) in 1928, "is a soft one, but it does not rest until it has gained a hearing. Ultimately, after endlessly repeated rebuffs, it succeeds. This is one of the viewpoints in which one may be optimistic about the future of mankind." Reason...speaks the language of all past times and places, which is the language of history.

AWARENESS OF THE HARM OF ANGER
AND VIOLENCE

You might think that anger and violence have obviously wreaked so much harm on individuals and communities that virtually everyone, including yourself, is fully aware of this and closely watches his reacting irately to others. Wrong! You may indeed have a general awareness of some of the disadvantages of rage, but how often do you focus on this and make yourself see exactly what harm will likely follow your enraging yourself? Very seldom, we would wager!

Let us briefly review some of the disadvantages of resentment and anger that you can think about:

Focusing on reprisal.   Although you ostensibly anger yourself to stop people from harming you and others, once you enrage yourself at these "wrongdoers" you tend to lose sight of their "dangerousness" and become obsessed with revenge.

Abuse of weaker individuals.   Anger and even righteous indignation may spur you to abuse some individuals who act poorly, including powerless children over whom you may, unfortunately, have control. As noted earlier, child abuse is an all too frequent occurrence in the United States.

Political violence.   Although the nations of the United Nations have so far managed to ward off another major holocaust like World War I or World War II, almost innumerable international and intranational conflicts continue to exist. Guerrilla warfare, hijackings, political murders, kidnappings, open warfare between political factions, and all kinds of bloodshed are common in virtually every part of the civilized and less civilized world today.

Religious warfare.   Just as political warfare stems from hatred of and bigotry against other groups, so does religious warfare. Religious strife is worldwide, including wars between Catholics and Protestants, Jews and Christians, Jews and Moslems, Moslems and Christians, Hindus and non-Hindus, etc. Each group, as usual, tends to believe that its views are right and that its opponent's views are demonically wrong—and that therefore, the opposing group has to be denounced, oppressed, and preferably annihilated. Even members of peace-loving groups, such as Jews and Christians, turn to bloodshed and murder when they violently anger themselves against members of other religious groups.

Prejudice against self and others.   Hatred of others often leads you to view them as devils incarnate and to magnify their "evil" traits. By attributing to them these traits, you frequently feel noble yourself—and then have to keep protecting your "nobility" by hating them more. As Marie Jahoda notes, "Despising others becomes a way of trying to bolster one's own shaky self-esteem by making others seem more inferior or contemptible. In fact, the only way some people can salvage their own self-respect is to feel 'lucky' they are not an African American, a Catholic, an Italian—or whoever is set up as the scapegoat for their own secret misery."

Taking on characteristics of those you hate.   Ironically, you tend to hate others for their poor characteristics—for their bullying, their prejudice, their violence, and their arrogance—and through hating them and justifying almost any action you can do to stop them, you frequently take on the very features that you loathe. If you thoroughly hate Hitler, you may turn into a Hitler—one who condemns others in their entirety because you dislike some of their traits. William Irwin Thompson points out that "we become what we hate" and notes that "in watching the conflict of the Irish Troubles, the Dublin yogi, George William Russell, developed the maxim into a principle of political science: 'By intensity of hatred nations create in themselves the characters they imagine in their enemies. Hence it is that all passionate conflicts result in the interchange of characteristics.'"

Increasing the trouble that injustice causes.   Paul Hauck, in *Overcoming Frustration and Anger*, rightly notes that making yourself angry when someone tries to "get your goat" only does you double injury:

> There are two statements I usually make to myself which help me keep my cool. The first is that I am not God and am neurotic to insist I have to have my way. This usually cools me off nicely. However, if that doesn't do the trick, I always throw in this next thought. "Hauck, be smart, someone is trying to shaft you. That's bad enough, old boy. Surely you're not going to be dumb now and do to yourself what that fellow is trying to do. No, sir! Maybe he doesn't give a hoot about my feelings, but I sure do. Therefore, I'm going to forcibly talk myself out of the angry mood which is beginning to come over me." Having trouble is one thing, and it's often unavoidable. But making *double trouble* for myself is another matter entirely.

Interference with activism.   Revolutionaries usually insist that only through making ourselves incensed at injustices can we propel ourselves into action to change poor social conditions. Partly true— and largely wrong! As Hannah Arendt has indicated, riots and rebellions often give their participants a false sense of action and tend to impede the careful planning, constructive action, and long-term follow-up procedures that would result in effective social change. Dramatic outbursts may at times lead to constructive reorganization, but they frequently do not. Outbursts, moreover, can continue for years and, if anything, block people from *doing* something about the execrable conditions against which they keep violently protesting.

Interference with the rights of others.   As Janet L. Wolfe points out, assertiveness differs from aggressiveness in that it consists of "the ability to express feelings or legitimate rights straightforwardly, without attacking others or violating their rights. Aggressive behavior, to the contrary, violates the rights of others, or puts them down." Rage, too, has an intrinsically fascistic or elitist philosophy behind it, for it denies the rights of others in favor of one's own "special" rights.

Interference with helping others to change.   The angrier you make yourself at others who hold opposing views and the more you express your fury, the less you tend to help them change their views and come around to yours. On the contrary, they usually feel more justified in opposing you and claiming that your rage *proves* you to be wrong. As David Burns notes, agreeing with your critics may help them be less critical of you. Violently disagreeing with them may increase their conviction that their accusations against you are valid.

CHALLENGING ANGRY ATTRIBUTIONS

When you are angry, you often tend to attribute horrible intentions to people who thwart you when they actually have no such intentions. Thus, a number of studies have shown that violent youths hold a "hostile attributional bias." They see intentional wrongdoing where none exists and go through life with an assume-the-worst attitude when faced by Adversities.

Watch this! If you tend to attribute vindictive motives to people who mistreat you, stop and question your assumptions and look for other possible reasons for this mistreatment.

In our illustration where Jack and Joan refuse to honor their apartment-sharing contract with you, if you are "certain" that they deliberately did you in, ask yourself: "Do I really *know* that they had this intention? Might they not have had *other* reasons for treating me unfairly? Could they, in their own lives, have had some *good* reasons for acting badly to me? Do I know all the facts or am I largely *assuming* several of them?"

Understanding attribution theory. When someone treats you in a certain way, particularly a frustrating or unfair way, you tend to attribute various motives to this person and to make yourself more or less angry accordingly. In recent years a number of social psychologists have pointed out the importance of attribution theory in understanding human feelings and actions. Russell Geen and David Stonner, for example, set up an experiment where male college students—after having seen a violent movie—could punish someone who had verbally attacked them. Under one set of experimental conditions the students learned that the movie fighting stemmed from professional or altruistic motives and under another set of conditions that it stemmed from revenge motives. The results showed that subjects led by the experimenters to attribute the fighting to revenge motives acted significantly more angrily and harshly toward the people whom they subsequently punished than did those who believed that the movie fighting stemmed from altruistic motives.

If you have a tendency—as you probably do—to attribute highly negative, vindictive motives to people who frustrate or attack you, *force yourself to stop and question your attributions* and try to see *other* possible reasons for the frustration or the attack. In the illustration where Jack and Joan renege on their promise to share an apartment with you, you may assume that:

1. They truly want to do you in.
2. They knew all along that they would never share the apartment with you and deliberately misled you.

Look for and check your attributions! Others frequently frustrate, annoy, and treat you unfairly. But only rarely do they do so because they hate you. Only occasionally do they *intend* to act vindictively toward you. In many instances, because of their own disturbances, they cannot easily help treating you badly, or they are unaware of their injustices to you, or they believe that they cannot possibly solve some of their own problems unless they deal with you unfairly. Seek, if you possibly can, their true motives and attitudes. And watch your exaggerated attributions!

REDUCING YOUR FEELINGS OF INADEQUACY

Many authorities note that feelings of hostility can seem immensely better than condemning oneself.

If you want to minimize anger that stems from your own feelings of insecurity, read over our early material and learn to stop damning yourself. Your traits, deeds, and performances may indeed be less than what you desire. Because you have some cards stacked against you, you may do decidedly worse in some respects than many other people. Too bad! Most unfortunate! Abysmally unfair! But if you really do have inferior traits or get looked down upon for what your social group wrongly defines as inferiorities, *you* still do not have to rate yourself as a lowly person and deem yourself unworthy of pleasure.

The more you accept yourself unconditionally—because you choose to remain alive and to strive for happiness, and for no other reason—the less tendency you will have to cover up your "inadequacy" with compensatory anger. This does not mean that you cannot rightly fight against social injustice or act as a rebel with a cause. You can! But try to do so because you want to right real wrongs and want to better your own life—and not to prove your strength or manliness or nobility. Who needs that kind of self-justification? Answer: people who first foolishly put themselves down.

AVOIDANCE OF DRUGS AND ALCOHOL

Studies of both anger-prone college students and adults have revealed high rates of drug and alcohol abuse. This goes two ways: Disturbed people are easily addicted to substances and often use drugs and alcohol as a way to deal with negative emotions; and problem drinkers and drug users lose control and have violent outbursts that they would often curb if they were not under the influence of these substances.

Alcohol and drug addicts, moreover, deal badly with life conditions, bring on unusual frustrations, and often make themselves addicted to low frustration tolerance and to needless anger. Alcohol frequently increases aggression–and experiments have shown that even the belief that you have consumed a considerable amount of liquor may result in aggressive behavior.

If you have a problem with anger, be careful about taking any alcohol or drugs. You may not have to abstain entirely. But closely watch your imbibing behavior.

A PHILOSOPHY OF FALLIBILITY

We can hardly overemphasize the point that all humans remain incredibly fallible and that this is their basic nature. Naturally, they can change and do better. But only within limits! They have just about no chance of always acting fair, just, ethical, right, or proper.

At the same time, you and other people are able to accept the fallibility of others and to forgive them for their crimes. An excellent case is that of Professor Anatol Hold of the University of Pennsylvania. When a young man in the city of Philadelphia sexually attacked and killed his three-and-a-half-year-old daughter, Hold wrote a remarkable letter to the *Philadelphia Bulletin* in which he said he hoped that the murderer would be brought to justice, psychologically treated, but *not* made to suffer the death penalty. For as much as he missed and grieved over his dead child, this father wrote, he fully acknowledged that the slayer was an exceptionally disturbed individual, driven to his deed by enormous feelings of inadequacy and worthlessness, and he could not, in all conscience, ask for the death of such a disordered person. Wrote Professor Hold: "My final word has to do with the operation of the machinery of justice. Had I caught the boy in the act, I would have wished to kill him. Now that there is no undoing of what has been done, I only wish to help him. Let no feelings of caveman vengeance influence us. Let us rather help him who did so human a thing."

In a remarkably similar case, Joseph Sturek, a mental health therapy aide at Central Islip State Hospital in New York, felt exceptionally sad when his sixteen-year-old son and several of his friends found Sturek's twelve-year-old daughter, Jennifer, who had been brutally murdered a few days before. But when evidence clearly showed that a fifteen-year-old boy, a neighbor of the Stureks, had committed the murder, Sturek said, "We must forgive the boy. He is very sick. Jennifer would have wanted us to forgive him."

Can you do anything to aid this kind of compassion in yourself and others? Yes—if you accept human fallibility, realize what harm revenge does, and fight against this human tendency to perpetuate rage.

Even though human aggression has strong biological elements, it doesn't have to prevail. We can teach our children to fight less. We can give them a head start in accepting and forgiving others. Don't expect miracles, because strong combative dispositions don't easily disappear. But if we can train "naturally" antagonistic animals, such as dogs and cats or cats and mice, to live together peacefully—which we definitely can—we can also encourage "naturally" antagonistic humans to behave much less assaultively. Why not try?

CURBING RIGHTEOUS INDIGNATION

"Righteous indignation" sounds great—because when you feel it you *absolutely know* that your opponents are wrong and you therefore are *entirely justified* in stopping them. And at all costs!

Well?

Well, actually not so well.

When your righteous indignation leads to extreme rage and violence—as it all too often may—stop and think before you give vent to it. Consider these important points:

1. Don't your opponents have *something* to their views? Look at *their* frame of reference. Is it really *completely* wrong? Always?

2. Even when you can find no good reasons for your adversary's views, don't they strongly *believe* that they are right? However deluded you may see them as being, haven't they the human right to be deluded?

3. Do you truly *understand* their "wrong" views? Have you listened to them carefully and checked to see if they are saying what you at first *think* they are saying? Would you still be indignant if you told them what you think they are contending, got them to agree that you are correct about your understanding of their position, and only then kept arguing with them?

4. Using REBT, show yourself that even if you are unquestionably right and your opponents are indubitably wrong, you don't *have* to prove this to them. It's not *necessary* that you correct and change them—however *desirable* it may be.

5. Assuming that your opponents are *absolutely* wrong—which is quite a dangerous assumption!—honestly acknowledge that your righteous indignation almost always has its own irrational elements. For when you strongly feel it, you are first "sanely" saying that your opponents' *acts* are very bad, which by usual standards may indeed be true. But you are also "insanely" raving that they *absolutely must not* act badly, are *wholly rotten people* when they do, and deserve *annihilation* for their atrocious deeds. So your righteous indignation is usually extreme rage that damns the sinners *and* their sins.

6. You can sometimes use REBT with your "evil" opponents by showing them that when they behave "wrong" they may be correctly fighting against "injustice" or "bad events" but that they are also incorrectly—and violently—upsetting themselves about these injustices or events, insisting that they *absolutely must not* exist, and going to extremes in opposing them. By using REBT in this manner you may be able to calm your opponents down and change their behavior. But don't count on this!

Nonviolence as a philosophy.   Violence as a philosophy has tended to rule the human kingdom. Only in a few notable cases has nonviolence been a planned, practical method of getting one's way without open warfare with one's opponents. Gandhi's prolonged fight to get the British to abdicate as the political ruler of India represents one such case.

As Christopher Lasch points out, the Indian doctrine of non-violence, or *Satyagraha*, assumes decency as latent in all people, as part of their very humanity: "To decide in advance that certain adversaries are incapable of decency is therefore to accuse them of inhumanity and to fall into precisely that arrogant moralizing from which Satyagraha proposes to deliver us in the first place."

Erik Erikson has nicely portrayed Gandhi's nonviolent approach. He points out that Gandhi's truth consists of the acceptance of the idea that violence against your adversaries really amounts to the same thing as violence against yourself. Martin Luther King Jr. subscribed to this same truth and wrote that "for practical as well as moral reasons, nonviolence offers the only road to freedom for my people. In violent warfare, one must be prepared to face ruthlessly the fact that there will be casualties by the thousands."

In your own life, you probably do not have to practice passive resistance or complete nonviolence against any barbaric horde. But you can, if you wish, show people that although you may often resist doing what they want you to do, you will do so in a nonviolent way. This prevents you from emotionally and physically upsetting yourself and may also set a good example to others and encourage peace on earth, goodwill to all people.

RECOGNIZING THE IRONY OF HATRED

Hatred can consume you more than almost any other feeling and, like jealousy and a few other passions, can obsess you and run your life. It goes far beyond feelings of frustration and brings with it an illusion of self-interest. On the surface, you seem absorbed in your own situation and *ostensibly* strive—through rage—to get what you want and to get rid of what you don't want. But what an illusion!

Feelings of anxiety—spurred by the Irrational Belief, "I must do well and win others' approval and it would be horrible if I didn't"!—make you other-directed rather than self-directed. But feelings of hatred have a similar effect. You can make yourself so furious about people who have treated you unfairly that you thereby make *them* the center of your attention and practically lose *yourself* in the process. You *seem* to want greater satisfaction for your own life, but you really obsess about changing *them*, doing *them* in, gloating over injury to *them*.

If you realize how other-directed this kind of thinking makes you, you can see how you defeat yourself by hating while deluding yourself that your hatred helps. You can then more easily go back to your main interest: "What, in view of the disadvantages of their treatment of me, can *I* do to make *my* life happier?" As Ken Olsen notes, "Hate is a means by which we punish and destroy ourselves for the actions of others." How ironic! See that you sink that irony into your brain many, many times—until you replace your hostility with self-interest integrated with social concern.

ACQUIRING HUMANISTIC VALUES

If you see yourself as part of the whole human race, if you acknowledge that all humans have a right to live and be happy, and if you see that your own life will most likely be more fulfilled if you act humanely to others, you will tend to feel much less angry and punishing even when others treat you shabbily. This does not mean that you have to go completely out of your way to help others or to sacrifice yourself for them. But it does mean that the more you acquire a humanistic set of values the less cruelly you will tend to treat other people.

To acquire a more humanistic philosophy, remember that you abhor needless mistreatment; that most people feel the same way; that concern for others tends to bring about the kind of conditions that you would like; and that treating others well in spite of their unfairness has challenging, self-growth elements. Without being a Florence Nightingale or St. Francis, you can find real satisfaction in trying to make the world a little better a place in which to live. Complete self-interest can become monotonous and boring. A vital, absorbing interest in something outside yourself, as REBT has shown since its inception, adds to long-range happiness. Devotion to a community or social cause helps you—as well as the human race.

REALIZING THE PAIN OF YOUR OPPONENTS

When angry, you tend to enjoy your own emotional outburst and to assume that somehow your targets will ultimately benefit from it. Fond hope! Your foes may well take your rage very badly, feel acute physical or emotional pain, or internalize your criticism and depress themselves. Vividly think about the pain that your opponents may experience and use these thoughts to inhibit your rage. What good does their anguish really do you?

Don't, of course, go to the other irrational extreme and condemn yourself for displaying anger. However mistaken and "rotten" your deed, you are never a *rotten person* for performing it. But your anger does have consequences—and, often, inhumane consequences to others who are vulnerable. Keep their vulnerability in mind. Try to see that even if their behavior has its evils, people do not really deserve to keep suffering—through your anger—because of it. Try to realize that their suffering will not necessarily eliminate their poor behavior.

ENHANCING YOUR RELATIONSHIPS

An obvious advantage of your not making yourself incensed at others is your enhancing your relationships with them under unangry conditions. Amazingly, however, you easily tend to forget this—and you concentrate on other dubious goals. As a parent, for example, you focus on teaching your children to do the right thing and insist that they *have to do* this. Consequently, when they do the wrong thing, you incense yourself at them—and scream that they'd better change. Result: you have poor relations with them and they do change—usually for the worse!

So remind yourself: "If I make myself angry at others, I will usually antagonize them and encourage them to keep acting badly.

If I accept them with their poor behavior and do not demand that they stop behaving that way, I will get along much better with them and also frequently serve as a more effective teacher. The less angry I feel, the more effective a teacher of the 'right way' I shall probably be. And the more friends I will have!"

COOPERATIVE OUTLOOK

REBT does not teach that competition is evil and that you should therefore avoid it. On the contrary, it assumes that you will often want to get what you want, to acquire more than others acquire, and to obtain things at others' expense.

Competition also applies to gaining someone else's approval or love. You want to establish an intimate relationship with someone and a rival also wants to establish an equally intimate relationship with him or her. The person you care for only desires monogamy, so either you or your competitor will lose out. Shall you withdraw from competition? Angrily fight with your competitor for the single "prize"? Obsessively plot and scheme to win the competition? What?

The usual REBT answer: Try, as strongly as you can, to get what you want and to win the competition, but don't insist that you must win it or else you will be a worthless slob and your opponent will be a villain. Determine—but not absolutely insist—on gaining what you want. At the same time, consider the advantage of a more cooperative outlook. Sometimes both you and your opponent can win, and you may even find it enjoyable to help him or her to achieve partial satisfaction. The goal you seek—whether love, money, or success—need not be your *only* preference. Sharing with others; cooperatively planning so that all of you may gain; feeling friendly toward your opponents—these aims may also be your goals.

Competition, remember, has disadvantages as well as gains. It takes time and effort. It encourages opposition from others. It overemphasizes winning. It has distinct social consequences for third parties—as when a union and management compete for industrial spoils and members of the public suffer from the ensuing strikes and lockouts. In a wider context, extreme competition can easily lead to international conflict and war.

In REBT terms, the more you train yourself to *want* but not to *need*, and the more you get yourself to cooperate with many individuals in your community rather than a small group of family members, the less angry you will feel.

You may not, of course, crave the satisfactions of cooperation and may therefore not work for them. But you have at least two viable options here, and the mere fact that you "naturally" have tended to favor one of them—one-sided competition—doesn't mean that you have to favor it forever.

WORKSHOPS, TRAINING COURSES, AND PSYCHOTHERAPY

In addition to using the REBT and CBT methods described in this book, you can of course work on improving your anger management skills by participating in seminars, workshops, training courses, and psychotherapy programs. But not any program! Some of the most popular workshops and therapies, especially those conducted by nonprofessional trainers, emphasize intense ventilation and acting out of your enraged feelings and can "help" you—and the people with whom you live and work—to become more furious than ever.

Workshops and therapies, however, that emphasize your making a cognitive-behavioral change and realizing and modifying your anger-creating philosophies—these may help you considerably. Also, you can benefit from programs that teach you specific behavioral skills, improved communication, healthy parenting techniques, etc. Try the methods described in this book and possibly explore and experiment with other training programs that show you how you are largely responsible for your anger and what you can specifically do to reduce it.

14

Accepting Yourself
With Your Anger

WE HOPE THIS BOOK HAS CLEARLY SHOWN YOU how you can minimize your anger and the other unhealthy feelings and actions that plague your everyday life. Because you remain a fallible human, however, you will from time to time find yourself slipping back into self-defeating attitudes and behaviors. So we'd better look at how you can best deal with yourself (and others) when this happens.

Let us say that you have successfully practiced several of the methods in this book. Yet just the other day your boss acted so nastily and unfairly toward you that you felt like really letting him have it. Fortunately, he had to leave the office before you had a chance to blow up in his presence, but even after he had gone, it took you more than half an hour to cool down. Your heart still pounds when you recall how vicious he was. Now let's see how you can deal better with your anger under those conditions.

First, you can fully acknowledge that you have enraged feelings against your boss rather than denying them or rationalizing them away; and you can admit that *you* mainly brought them on and that *you* are foolishly reliving them. You made yourself angry—your boss didn't. And you did so wrongly, stupidly. You rightly felt annoyed and irritated at his presumably nasty and overly critical behavior. Why should you like it when it was so unfair? But you then angered yourself *about* his nastiness and his unfairness—which you didn't have to do.

Second, and perhaps even more important, you can work at accepting yourself *with* your rage. You can acknowledge the wrongness of your feelings but not the badness of you. See that like other people, you may act badly, but you don't have to condemn yourself for acting that way. As a fallible human person, you give yourself the right to be wrong, to make yourself unhealthily angry. Show yourself that you aren't an idiot or a worm for doing so. You are merely a *person who* has acted stupidly—not a stupid *person*.

Say to yourself something like, "I really behaved self-defeatingly in incensing myself at my boss, but I can easily do so and have a right, as a human, to act that silly way. My acts are wrong, but I *am not* a really rotten person." In other words, accept yourself while *not* accepting your behavior. Fully acknowledge its stupidity: that it most likely brings you more harm than good.

Review your anger and see why it does you harm. It gives you a "pain in the gut." It doesn't help you solve your problem with your boss. It easily may make your relationship with him much worse. It may lead to physical problems (high blood pressure, etc.). It makes you preoccupied with your boss and his apparent irrationality, keeping you from focusing on how to do your job better and please him more. It sabotages your efficiency in many ways.

If you feel determined to accept *you*, your humanity, in spite of your anger, you will have little trouble in fully acknowledging *it* as bad or self-sabotaging. But if you insist on condemning yourself, your totality, for your anger, then you will tend to deny, repress, and excuse your rage. And you will find yourself dealing poorly with it. Look at it as bad but correctable!

Review what you mistakenly told yourself to make yourself angry. Resolve to think something different in the future—and practice doing so in your head. You can now see that you *demanded* that your boss act nicely and fairly and that when he didn't fulfill this demand, you told yourself, "How awful! He has no right to act the way I don't want him to! I can't stand his stupidity! I hope he drops dead!"

Now you ask yourself—at D for Disputing—"Why is it *awful* for my boss to act nastily and unfairly? Why has he *no right* to act that way? Prove that I really *can't stand* his stupidity. Is he really a *total villain* who should drop dead to please me?"

You can answer: "*Nothing* makes it awful for my boss to act nastily and unfairly. It's only annoying and inconvenient! He *does* have the right to act any way that he acts. Even though he behaves wrongly and I don't like his behavior, I *can* definitely stand it. I certainly am not a villain when I wrongly displease him. So neither is he when he displeases me!"

Note that by approaching the situation through using the ABC's of REBT, you have not chosen to feel irresponsible about your fury at your boss, thereby encouraging your future fury. You have honestly acknowledged your anger—and acknowledged *its* wrongness. You have made an attempt to understand what *you* did to make yourself angry and what *you* can do in the future to stop making yourself enraged again. That is the main point. You live successfully with your anger by *understanding* it. By realistically seeing that humans easily and naturally make themselves angry. By *accepting* yourself for creating it. By *showing yourself how to Dispute it.*

Once you start acknowledging and Disputing the Irrational Beliefs that largely create rage, you can follow certain practical procedures that will let you get some of your steam off harmlessly and perhaps also encourage those at whom you feel angry to reconsider their own behavior. Here are several things you can do:

1. Try to assert yourself to the people at whom you feel angry in I-statements rather than in you-statements. If you hate your boss for making you work overtime and not compensating you, don't say to him, "You keep treating me unfairly by making me work overtime! I don't understand how you can do that!" Such a statement directly accuses him of "vile" behavior and assumes that he knows how bad it is and therefore *absolutely should not* do it. Your accusation will hardly encourage him to listen to you nicely.

Instead, you can give the same message in the following kind of I-statement: "I feel that I keep getting asked to work overtime without additional compensation, and I don't like that. I wonder whether this is fair. Assuming that from my point of view it has an unfair element, I wonder how you see it from your point of view." This kind of I-statement shows your feelings and shows that you think of something as wrong, but it does so diplomatically. It reveals your displeasure, but not your immense anger—even if you happen to feel angry while saying it.

2. When you feel angry at people who don't seem aware of the "bad" way they have acted, try to speak authoritatively rather than authoritarianly. If, for example, you have an employee who keeps coming in late, you don't have to say, "How can you do that all the time? You know darned well that we don't tolerate any lateness here!" You can say instead, "I don't know whether anyone pointed it out to you clearly when you joined this firm, but we have a strict policy about lateness. Anyone who comes even a few minutes late several times gets talked to by his or her supervisor and is penalized if he or she does not start coming on time. The company has had this rule for a long time and finds it advisable to stick to it. So I have called you in to talk about the problem of your lateness."

Or if you notice that a classmate keeps asking to borrow your homework in order to copy it and you feel angry about this, you can say something like: "Maybe you don't agree with the homework rule and think it silly. But I have personally found that I really don't understand what goes on in class unless I regularly do my homework. It seems to me that the best way to learn this subject is to practice it on one's own. So I feel that lending you my homework to copy won't really do you much good and that you'd do yourself a disservice by using it. Therefore, I don't think I will lend it to you." This kind of response seems much better than your authoritarianly telling the attempted borrower, "Look, dear! You just don't borrow homework in this class. That won't do at all!"

3. Usually you will get along better if, when someone puts you down and you feel angry about it, you refrain from following suit and lambasting her. Such a vengeful retort will often make you feel better—but not get better results. It will tend to make you feel more angry, and you will win the other's enmity. So your best retort frequently consists of seeming to agree with the put-down, ignoring

it, agreeing with it in part, or showing the other person that you do not take it too seriously, do not agree with it, and can firmly but calmly respond.

If an acquaintance of yours, for example, laughs at you for dressing in a certain manner, you can make these kinds of retorts: (a) "Yes, my jacket does seem on the loud side." (b) "I see that you really don't like the way I dress." (c) "I guess my jacket does seem on the loud side but I find it exciting and attractive." (d) "I can see what you mean and that others might agree with you, but I don't consider things like this that important." (e) "Apparently we just don't agree on what constitutes loudness." (f) "You may think it's loud, but almost everyone seems to wear this kind of color these days, and therefore even if you're right I think I'll go along with the crowd."

With these kinds of retorts, you hold your ground but do not rage at others. Even when you feel angry as you respond in this way, your responses tend to calm you down and make you feel somewhat less irate. You never lose integrity by acting this way, for even if your acquaintance thinks that you are weak, that may be her problem, and you need never feel like an inferior person.

4. As Herbert Fensterheim and Jean Baer rightly point out, this does not mean that you had better be apologetic or self-loathing when someone puts you down and you feel angry. If someone criticizes your taste in a jacket, you do not reply, "Yes, I guess people do think less of me when I wear loud colors like this," or "You're right. I must have very poor taste." Acting weakly may encourage your critic to try to put you down further and may set a bad example for others. As I (AE) have stated in *How to Live With a "Neurotic,"* try an attitude of firm kindness. Not unfirm kindness; not firm unkindness. Simply firm kindness—and the maintaining of your own integrity no matter what others may think of you.

5. Occasionally, you will find it best to retort to put-downs in a sarcastic, mean, or critical manner. For in certain groups—such as tough street-corner gangs—if you don't stand up for yourself and return unkindness in kind, the group may view you as weak and may repeatedly victimize you. Make sarcastic retorts the exception rather

than the rule, however, even when others have clearly insulted you and you feel angry about this.

6. Don't be perfectionistic about your dealing with your anger and replying "properly" to people when you feel angry at them. Inevitably, you will at times retort badly or weakly, and sometimes you will make yourself so incensed that you will reply to people in an extremely bottled-up, chokingly furious manner. So you will! It would be lovely if you always handled yourself beautifully when angry and did not act foolishly. But you *will* act that way at times. You darned well will!

Learn to accept yourself with your weakness—as well as with your anger. Your stupidity merely shows your humanity. (Leonardo da Vinci, Isaac Newton, and Albert Einstein frequently acted idiotically. And so do you.)

7. See that you can make yourself less angry. Perfect lack of hostility you will never achieve, but you can make yourself less frequently and less intently irate. Try, and don't give up too easily. Give yourself practice at talking yourself out of your rage, and try, at the same time, to talk some of your close friends and associates out of some of theirs. If you can show them how to feel less enraged, they may serve as good examples for the reduction of your own hostility.

8. When you do feel angry, try to acknowledge this to both yourself and others. Not always, of course! If you feel exceptionally angry at your school principal or at one of your bosses, you'd better pretend that you don't. But not with your friends and associates— with whom you can be fairly honest. Admit how angry you feel— and admit to yourself that *you* made yourself angry. You will then avoid the problem of squelching your anger, keeping it under strong wraps, and thereby consuming time and energy that you can better spend in facing it and doing something to reduce it.

If you want to live successfully with your anger, do some of the same things that you would do if you wanted to minimize it. REBT methods work in much the same way whether you want to reduce emotional disturbance or live more happily while you still experience it. Paul A. Hauck, in an REBT book, *Overcoming Frustration and Anger*, gives several good rules for avoiding hostility that can also help if you still make yourself angry and want to survive happily while you try to lessen your rage.

Hauck points out, for example, that righteous indignation gives you no good excuse to remain angry, for all anger tends to include righteousness: "In fact, anger wouldn't arise in the first place if you didn't think you were completely right in your opinion and that the other person was completely wrong. That even applies to things and nature. When you give your flat tire an angry kick you really are trying to tell the world that that tire had no right to go flat on you, that it has done a mean and dirty trick, and that it deserves a kick for being such a lousy tire."

Recognizing your righteous indignation and facing some of its foolishness will help you stop kicking the tire—and also help you humorously acknowledge it and accept it as part of your very fallible all-too-human condition.

REBT, along with Paul Hauck and Bud Nye, recommends that you can constructively make yourself angry at people's *acts* but not at the *actors*. Including yourself as an actor! If you feel highly displeased at serious deficiencies, you may encourage yourself and others to correct these failings, and thereby fulfill the constructive aspects of your nature. Strong criticism can lead to productive problem-solving—if it is nondamning.

Hauck continues his book, *Overcoming Frustration and Anger*, with this REBT proverb, "*Forgive everything* and *forget nothing*." Nicely stated! If, for example, you forgive Joan and Jack for unfairly backing out of their promise to share an apartment with you, and if you accept them as humans *with* rotten behavior, you can remember this unfortunate experience and use it to protect yourself from similar injustices in the future. You can then live more successfully with your anger at Jack and Joan's (and other people's) *acts* while surrendering your rage at *them*.

15

A Few Concluding Remarks

ALL OF THE MANY METHODS OF REDUCING RAGE and of living successfully with your still remaining anger work beautifully—with some of the people some of the time. None of them is perfect. All have their limitations. You, as a unique individual, will find some of them remarkably effective—and some lukewarm. What can you do but actively experiment with them? Very little!

Can these clinically and scientifically tested anger-reducing methods specifically help you to feel less enraged and to live better and to suffer less when, for all your efforts, you still act angrily? Most probably, yes, provided that you accept our main REBT thesis: that as a human being you often take serious problems and injustices—many of which you don't create—and you do create needless rages about them.

Once you accept your own part in fabricating anger—not to mention other disturbed feelings—you are well on the way to using your natural problem-solving and happiness-enhancing tendencies. You can then focus on solving life's difficulties instead of unhinging yourself about them. Once you see that although rage seems to control you, you have remarkable power to control and reduce it, you can train yourself to be much less angry.

You may find that you don't even have to go that far. As we have noted, you can learn to live fairly happily *with* your anger. If you wish, you can stop right there. You don't *have* to make yourself unangry almost every time your anger rises. You can accept yourself with your resentful feelings and help yourself considerably by this very acceptance. You will often find, however, that when you start to reach this stage, when you stubbornly refuse to condemn yourself when you feel angry and when you look more at problem-solving and less at the "horrible" unfairness of life, you will probably want to go on to the next and more elegant step— surrendering your anger for a more forgiving, less damning attitude toward the world and the people in it. Not that you have to. But why not try it and see?

Appendix

REBT Self-Help Form

A (ACTIVATING EVENT)

- Briefly summarize the situation you are disturbed about (what would a camera see?)
- An *A* can be *internal* or *external, real* or *imagined.*
- An *A* can be an event in the *past, present,* or *future.*

IB's (IRRATIONAL BELIEFS)   ## D (DISPUTING IB'S)

To identify IB's, look for:

- DOGMATIC DEMANDS
  (musts, absolutes, shoulds)

- AWFULIZING
  (It's awful, terrible, horrible)

- LOW FRUSTRATION TOLERANCE
  (I can't stand it)

- SELF/OTHER RATING
  (I'm / he / she is bad, worthless)

To dispute ask yourself:

- Where is holding this belief getting me? Is it *helpful* or *self-defeating*?
- Where is the evidence to support the existence of my irrational belief? Is it *consistent with reality*?
- Is my belief *logical*? Does it follow from my preferences?
- Is it really *awful* (as bad as it could be?)
- Can I really not *stand* it?

© *Windy Dryden & Jane Walker 1992. Revised by Albert Ellis Institute, 1996.*

C (CONSEQUENCES)

Major unhealthy negative **emotions:**

Major self-defeating **behaviors:**

Unhealthy negative emotions include:
- Anxiety
- Depression
- Rage
- Low Frustration Tolerance
- Shame/Embarassment
- Hurt
- Jealousy
- Guilt

RB's (RATIONAL BELIEFS)   ## E (NEW EFFECT)

New healthy
negative emotions:

New constructive
behaviors:

To think more rationally, strive for:

- NON-DOGMATIC PREFERENCES
  (wishes, wants, desires)

- EVALUATING BADNESS
  (it's bad, unfortunate)

- HIGH FRUSTRATION TOLERANCE
  (I don't like it, but I can stand it)

- NOT GLOBALLY RATING SELF OR
  OTHERS (I—and others—are fallible
  human beings)

Healthy negative emotions include:

- Disappointment

- Concern

- Annoyance

- Sadness

- Regret

- Frustration

A (ACTIVATING EVENT)

> My boss criticized Me severely
> and Treated Me unfairly

- Briefly summarize the situation you are disturbed about (what would a camera see?)
- An *A* can be *internal* or *external*, *real* or *imagined*.
- An *A* can be an event in the *past*, *present*, or *future*.

IB's (IRRATIONAL BELIEFS)

> He Never should
> Treat Me That Way!
> I can't stand his
> Unfair Treatment!
> He's a very Nasty
> and rotten person!

D (DISPUTING IB'S)

> Where is The evidence
> That my boss must
> Treat Me fairly?
> Does it follow That
> because his Treatment
> of Me is unfair
> I can't stand it and
> cannot be happy
> at all?
> Does his bad Treatment
> Make him a Totally
> rotten person?
> Will holding my
> irrational Beliefs
> help or hinder me?

To identify IB's, look for:

- DOGMATIC DEMANDS (musts, absolutes, shoulds)
- AWFULIZING (It's awful, terrible, horrible)
- LOW FRUSTRATION TOLERANCE (I can't stand it)
- SELF/OTHER RATING (I'm / he / she is bad, worthless)

To dispute ask yourself:

- Where is holding this belief getting me? Is it *helpful* or *self-defeating*?
- Where is the evidence to support the existence of my irrational belief? Is it *consistent with reality*?
- Is my belief *logical*? Does it follow from my preferences?
- Is it really *awful* (as bad as it could be?)
- Can I really not *stand* it?

© *Windy Dryden & Jane Walker 1992. Revised by Albert Ellis Institute, 1996.*

C (CONSEQUENCES)

> **Major unhealthy negative emotions:**
> Anger
>
> **Major self-defeating behaviors:**
> Stayed out of work for three days and sulked

Unhealthy negative emotions include:
- Anxiety
- Depression
- Rage
- Low Frustration Tolerance
- Shame/Embarassment
- Hurt
- Jealousy
- Guilt

RB's (RATIONAL BELIEFS)

There is no evidence that my boss must treat me fairly. Even though his treatment is unfair I can stand it and still experience happiness. His bad treatment of me makes him a person who can treat people badly — but because he does many other things he is never a totally bad person. Holding my irrational belief will not change him, make me enraged, and encourage him to treat me worse.

To think more rationally, strive for:

- NON-DOGMATIC PREFERENCES (wishes, wants, desires)
- EVALUATING BADNESS (it's bad, unfortunate)
- HIGH FRUSTRATION TOLERANCE (I don't like it, but I can stand it)
- NOT GLOBALLY RATING SELF OR OTHERS (I—and others—are fallible human beings)

E (NEW EFFECT)

New healthy negative emotions:
Disappointment and frustration.

New constructive behaviors:
Confront my boss unangrily and assertively.

Healthy negative emotions include:

- Disappointment
- Concern
- Annoyance
- Sadness
- Regret
- Frustration

Selected References

Note: The items preceded by an asterisk (*) in the following list of references are recommended for readers who want to obtain more details about Rational Emotive Behavior Therapy (REBT) and Cognitive Behavior Therapy (CBT). Those preceded by two asterisks (**) are REBT and CBT self-help books and materials. Many of these materials are obtainable from the Albert Ellis Institute, 45 East 65th Street, New York, NY 10021-6508. The Institute's free catalog and the materials it distributes may be ordered on weekdays by phone (212-535-0822) or by fax (212-249-3582). In addition to these and other materials, the Institute offers talks, workshops, and training sessions, as well as other presentations in the area of human growth and healthy living, and lists these in its catalog. Many of the references listed here are not referred to in the text, especially a number of the self-help materials.

*Abrams, M., and Ellis, A. (1994). "Rational Emotive Behavior Therapy in the Treatment of Stress." *British Journal of Guidance and Counseling*, 22 (pp. 39–50).

**Alberti, R. F., and Emmons, M. L. (1995). *Your Perfect Right*, 7th rev. ed. San Luis Obispo, CA: Impact.

*Ansbacher, H. L., and Ansbacher, R. (1956). *The Individual Psychology of Alfred Adler*. New York: Basic Books.

Averill, J.R. (1983). "Studies on Anger and Aggression: Implications for Theories of Emotion." *American Psychologist* 38 (pp. 1145–60).

Bach, G. R., and Goldberg, H. (1975). *Creative Aggressions*. New York: Avon.

**Baldon, A., and Ellis, A. (1993). *RET Problem Solving Workbook*. New York: Institute for Rational-Emotive Therapy.

*Bandura, A. (1986). *Social Foundations of Thought and Action: A Social Cognitive Theory*. Englewood Cliffs, NJ: Prentice-Hall.

*Barlow, D. H. (1989). *Anxiety and Its Disorders: The Nature and Treatment of Anxiety and Panic*. New York: Guilford.

**Barlow, D. H., and Craske, M. G. (1994). *Mastery of Your Anxiety and Panic*. San Antonio, TX: The Psychological Corporation.

*Beck, A. T. (1976). *Cognitive Therapy and the Emotional Disorders*. New York: International Universities Press.

**_____(1988). *Love Is Not Enough*. New York: Harper & Row.

*Beck, A. T., and Emery, G. (1985). *Anxiety Disorders and Phobias*. New York: Basic Books.

*Beck, J. S. (1995). *Cognitive Therapy: Basics and Beyond*. New York: Guilford.

*Bernard, M. E., ed. (1991). *Using Rational-Emotive Therapy Effectively: A Practitioner's Guide*. New York: Plenum.

**_____(1993). *Staying Rational in an Irrational World*. New York: Carol Publishing.

*Bernard, M. E., and DiGiuseppe, R., eds. (1989). *Inside RET: A Critical Appraisal of the Theory and Therapy of Albert Ellis*. San Diego, CA: Academic Press.

*Bernard, M. E., and Wolfe, J. L., eds. (1993). *The RET Resource Book for Practitioners*. New York: Institute for Rational-Emotive Therapy.

*Blau, S. F. (1993). "Cognitive Darwinism: Rational-Emotive Therapy and the Theory of Neuronal Group Selection." *ETC: A Review of General Semantics* 50 (pp. 403–41).

**Bloomfield, H. H., and McWilliams, P. (1994). *How to Heal Depression*. Los Angeles: Prelude Press.

Boorstin, D. J. (1970, July 6). "A Case of Hypochondria." *Newsweek* (pp. 27–29).

**Broder, M. S. (1994). *The Art of Staying Together*. New York: Avon.

**Broder, M. (Speaker) (1995a). *Overcoming Your Anger in the Shortest Period of Time*. Cassette recording. New York: Institute for Rational-Emotive Therapy.

**_____(Speaker) (1995b). *Overcoming Your Anxiety in the Shortest Period of Time*. Cassette recording. New York: Institute for Rational-Emotive Therapy.

**_____(Speaker) (1995c). *Overcoming Your Depression in the Shortest Period of Time*. Cassette recording. New York: Institute for Rational-Emotive Therapy.

**Burns, D. D. (1980). *Feeling Good: The New Mood Therapy*. New York: Morrow.

**_____(1989). *The Feeling Good Handbook*. New York: Plume.

**_____(1993). *Ten Days to Self-Esteem*. New York: Morrow.

Cannon, W. B. (1932). *The Wisdom of the Body*. New York: Norton.

**Covey, S. R. (1992). *The Seven Habits of Highly Effective People*. New York: Simon & Schuster.

*Crawford, T., and Ellis, A. (1989). "A Dictionary of Rational-Emotive

Feelings and Behaviors." *Journal of Rational-Emotive and Cognitive-Behavioral Therapy* 7 (1) (pp. 3–27).

**Danysh, J. (1974). *Stop Without Quitting*. San Francisco: International Society for General Semantics.

Davis, M., Eshelman, E. R., and McKay, M. (1988). *The Relaxation and Stress Reduction Workbook*. Oakland, CA: New Harbinger Publications.

*Deffenbacher, J. (1995). "Ideal Treatment Package for Adults With Anger Disorders." In H. Kassinove, ed., *Anger Disorders: Definition, Diagnosis, and Treatment* (pp. 151–72). Washington, D.C.: Taylor and Francis.

Deffenbacher, J. L., and Stark, R. S. (1992). "Relaxation and Cognitive-Relaxation Treatments of General Anger." *Journal of Counseling Psychology* 39 (2) (pp. 158–67).

**DiGiuseppe, R. (Speaker) (1990). *What Do I Do With My Anger: Hold It In or Let It Out?* Cassette recording. New York: Institute for Rational-Emotive Therapy.

*———(1991a). "Comprehensive Cognitive Disputing in RET." In M. E. Bernard, ed., *Using Rational-Emotive Therapy Effectively* (pp. 173–96). New York: Plenum.

**———(Speaker) (1991b). *Maximizing the Moment: How to Have More Fun and Happiness in Life*. Cassette recording. New York: Institute for Rational-Emotive Therapy.

*DiGiuseppe, R., Tafrate, R., and Eckhardt, C. (1994). "Critical Issues in the Treatment of Anger." *Cognitive and Behavioral Practice* 1 (pp. 111-32).

DiMattia, D. (1991). *Rational Effectiveness Training*. New York: Institute for Rational-Emotive Therapy.

DiMattia, D., and Ijzermans, T. (1996). *Reaching Their Minds: A Trainer's Manual for Rational Effectiveness Training* New York: Institute for Rational-Emotive Therapy.

*DiMattia, D., and Lega, L., eds. (1990). *Will the Real Albert Ellis Please Stand Up? Anecdotes by His Colleagues, Students and Friends Celebrating His 75th Birthday*. New York: Institute for Rational-Emotive Therapy.

**DiMattia, D. J., and others (Speakers). (1987). *Mind Over Myths: Handling Difficult Situations in the Workplace*. Cassette recording. New York: Institute for Rational-Emotive Therapy.

Dolnick, E. (1995) "Hotheads and Heart Attacks." *Health*. July/August (pp. 58–64).

*Dryden, W. (1990). *Dealing With Anger Problems: Rational-Emotive Therapeutic Interventions*. Sarasota, FL: Professional Resource Exchange.

**———(1994). *Overcoming Guilt!* London: Sheldon.

*———(1995a). *Brief Rational-Emotive Behavior Therapy*. London: Wiley.

*_____, ed. (1995b). *Rational Emotive Behavior Therapy: A Reader*. London: Sage.

*Dryden, W., Backx, W., and Ellis, A. (1987). "Problems in Living: The Friday Night Workshop." In W. Dryden, *Current Issues in Rational-Emotive Therapy* (pp.154–70). London and New York: Croom Helm.

*Dryden, W., and DiGiuseppe, R. (1990). *A Primer on Rational-Emotive Therapy*. Champaign, IL: Research Press.

*Dryden, W., and Ellis, A. (1989). Albert Ellis: "An Efficient and Passionate Life. *Journal of Counseling and Development* 67 (pp. 539–46). New York: Institute for Rational-Emotive Therapy.

**Dryden, W., and Gordon, J. (1991). *Think Your Way to Happiness*. London: Sheldon Press.

**_____(1993). *Peak Performance*. Oxfordshire, England: Mercury.

*Dryden, W., and Hill, L. K., eds. (1993). *Innovations in Rational-Emotive Therapy*. Newbury Park, CA: Sage.

*Dryden, W., and Neenan, M. (1995). *Dictionary of Rational Emotive Behavior Therapy*. London: Whurr Publishers.

*Dryden, W., and Yankura, J. (1992). *Daring to Be Myself: A Case Study in Rational-Emotive Therapy*. Buckingham, England, and Philadelphia, PA: Open University Press.

*_____(1994). *Albert Ellis*. London: Sage.

**Ellis, A. (1957). *How to Live With a "Neurotic": At Home and at Work*. New York: Crown. Rev. ed., Hollywood, CA: Wilshire Books, 1975.

**_____(1972a). *Executive Leadership: The Rational-Emotive Approach*. New York: Institute for Rational-Emotive Therapy.

*_____(1972b). "Helping People Get Better Rather Than Merely Feel Better." *Rational Living* 7 (2) (pp. 2–9).

**_____(1972c). *How to Master Your Fear of Flying*. New York: Institute for Rational-Emotive Therapy.

**_____(Speaker) (1973a). *How to Stubbornly Refuse to Be Ashamed of Anything*. Cassette recording. New York: Institute for Rational-Emotive Therapy.

*_____(1973b). *Humanistic Psychotherapy: The Rational-Emotive Approach*. New York: McGraw-Hill.

**_____(Speaker) (1973c). *Twenty-one Ways to Stop Worrying*. Cassette recording. New York: Institute for Rational-Emotive Therapy.

**_____(Speaker) (1974). *Rational Living in an Irrational World*. Cassette recording. New York: Institute for Rational-Emotive Therapy.

*_____(1976a). "The Biological Basis of Human Irrationality." *Journal of Individual Psychology* 32 (pp. 145–68). Reprinted: New York: Institute for Rational-Emotive Therapy.

**_____(Speaker) (1976b). *Conquering Low Frustration Tolerance*. Cassette recording. New York: Institute for Rational-Emotive Therapy.

**_____(Speaker) (1977a). *Conquering the Dire Need For Love*. Cassette recording. New York: Institute for Rational-Emotive Therapy.

*_____(1977b). "Fun as Psychotherapy." *Rational Living* 12 (1) (pp. 2–6). Also: Cassette recording. New York: Institute for Rational-Emotive Therapy.

**_____(Speaker) (1977c). *A Garland of Rational Humorous Songs*. Cassette recording and song book. New York: Institute for Rational-Emotive Therapy.

**_____(1978). *I'd Like to Stop But…Dealing With Addictions*. Cassette recording. New York: Institute for Rational-Emotive Therapy.

**_____(1979a). *The Intelligent Woman's Guide to Dating and Mating*. Secaucus, NJ: Lyle Stuart.

*_____(1979b). "Rational-Emotive Therapy: Research Data That Support the Clinical and Personality Hypotheses of RET and Other Modes of Cognitive-Behavior Therapy." In A. Ellis and J. M. Whiteley, eds., *Theoretical and Empirical Foundations of Rational-Emotive Therapy* (pp. 101–73). Monterey, CA: Brooks/Cole.

**_____(Speaker) (1980c). *Twenty-two Ways to Brighten Up Your Love Life*. Cassette recording. New York: Institute for Rational-Emotive Therapy.

**_____(Speaker) (1982). *Solving Emotional Problems*. Cassette recording. New York: Institute for Rational-Emotive Therapy.

*_____(1985a). *Intellectual Fascism*. New York: Institute for Rational-Emotive Therapy. Rev. 1991.

*_____(1985b). *Overcoming Resistance: Rational-Emotive Therapy With Difficult Clients*. New York: Springer.

*_____(1987a). "The Evolution of Rational-Emotive Therapy (RET) and Cognitive-Behavior Therapy (CBT)." In J. K. Zeig, ed., *The Evolution of Psychotherapy* (pp. 107–32). New York: Brunner/Mazel.

*_____(1987b). "A Sadly Neglected Cognitive Element in Depression." *Cognitive Therapy and Research* 11 (pp. 121–46).

*_____(1987c). "The Use of Rational Humorous Songs in Psychotherapy." In W. F. Fry Jr. and W. A. Salamed, eds., *Handbook of Humor and Psychotherapy* (pp. 265–87). Sarasota, FL: Professional Resource Exchange.

*_____(1988a). *How to Stubbornly Refuse to Make Yourself Miserable About Anything—Yes, Anything!* Secaucus, NJ: Lyle Stuart.

**_____(Speaker) (1988b). *Unconditionally Accepting Yourself and Others*. Cassette recording. New York: Institute for Rational-Emotive Therapy.

*_____(1989a). "Comments on My Critics." In M. E. Bernard and R. DiGiuseppe, eds., *Inside Rational-Emotive Therapy* (pp. 199–233). San Diego, CA: Academic Press.

*_____(1989b). "The History of Cognition in Psychotherapy." In A. Freeman, K. M. Simon, L. E. Beutler, and H. Aronowitz, eds., *Comprehensive Handbook of Cognitive Therapy* (pp. 5–19). New York: Plenum.

**_____(Speaker) (1990a). *Albert Ellis Live at the Learning Annex.* Cassette recording. New York: Institute for Rational-Emotive Therapy.

*_____(1990b). "My Life in Clinical Psychology." In C. E. Walker, ed., *History of Clinical Psychology in Autobiography* (pp. 1–37). Homewood, IL: Dorsey.

*_____(1991a). "Achieving Self-Actualization." *Journal of Social Behavior and Personality* 6 (5) (pp. 1–18). Reprinted, New York: Institute for Rational-Emotive Therapy, 1993.

**_____(Speaker) (1991b). *How to Get Along With Difficult People.* Cassette recording. New York: Institute for Rational-Emotive Therapy.

**_____(Speaker) (1991c). *How to Refuse to Be Angry, Vindictive, and Unforgiving.* Cassette recording. New York: Institute for Rational-Emotive Therapy.

*_____(1991d). "The Revised ABCs of Rational-Emotive Therapy." In J. Zeig, ed., *The Evolution of Psychotherapy: The Second Conference* (pp. 79–99). New York: Brunner/Mazel. Expanded version: *Journal of Rational-Emotive and Cognitive-Behavior Therapy*, 1991, 9 (pp. 139–72).

**_____(1991e). *Self-Management Workbook: Strategies for Personal Success.* New York: Institute for Rational-Emotive Therapy.

*_____(1991f). "Using RET Effectively: Reflections and Interview." In M. E. Bernard, ed., *Using Rational-Emotive Therapy Effectively* (pp. 1–33). New York: Plenum.

*_____(1992a). "Brief Therapy: The Rational-Emotive Method." In S. H. Budman, M. F. Hoyt, and S. Fiedman, eds., *The First Session in Brief Therapy* (pp. 36–58). New York: Guilford.

**_____(1992b). Foreword to Paul Hauck, *Overcoming the Rating Game* (pp. 1–4). Louisville, KY: Westminster/John Knox.

**_____(Speaker) (1992c). *How to Age With Style.* Cassette recording. New York: Institute for Rational-Emotive Therapy.

*_____(1992d). "Group Rational-Emotive and Cognitive-Behavioral Therapy." *International Journal of Group Psychotherapy* 42 (pp. 63–80).

*_____(1993a). "The Advantages and Disadvantages of Self-Help Therapy Materials." *Professional Psychology: Research and Practice* 24 (pp. 335–39).

*_____(1993b). "Changing Rational-Emotive Therapy (RET) to Rational

Emotive Behavior Therapy (REBT)." *Behavior Therapist* 16 (pp. 257–58).

*_____(Speaker) (1993c). *Coping With the Suicide of a Loved One.* Video-cassette. New York: Institute for Rational-Emotive Therapy.

*_____(1993d). "Fundamentals of Rational-Emotive Therapy for the 1990s." In W. Dryden and L. K. Hill, eds., *Innovations in Rational-Emotive Therapy* (pp. 1–32). Newbury Park, CA: Sage Publications.

*_____(1993e). "General Semantics and Rational-Emotive Behavior Therapy." *Bulletin of General Semantics* 58 (pp. 12–28). Also in P. D. Johnston, D. D. Bourland Jr., and J. Klein, eds., *More E-Prime* (pp. 213–40). Concord, CA: International Society for General Semantics.

**_____(Speaker) (1993f). *How to Be a Perfect Non-Perfectionist.* Cassette recording. New York: Institute for Rational-Emotive Therapy.

**_____(Speaker) (1993g). *Living Fully and in Balance: This Isn't a Dress Rehearsal—This Is It!* Cassette recording. New York: Institute for Rational-Emotive Therapy.

*_____(1993h). "Rational Emotive Imagery: RET Version." In M. E. Bernard and J. L. Wolfe, eds., *The RET Source Book for Practitioners* (pp. II8–II10). New York: Institute for Rational-Emotive Therapy.

*_____(1993i). "The Rational-Emotive Therapy (RET) Approach to Marriage and Family Therapy." *Family Journal: Counseling and Therapy for Couples and Families* 1 (pp. 292–307).

*_____(1993j). "Reflections on Rational-Emotive Therapy." *Journal of Consulting and Clinical Psychology* 61 (pp. 199–201).

**_____(Speaker) (1993k). *Releasing Your Creative Energy.* Cassette recording. New York: Institute for Rational-Emotive Therapy.

*_____(1993l). "Vigorous RET Disputing." In M. E. Bernard and J. L. Wolfe, eds., *The RET Resource Book for Practitioners* (pp. II7). New York: Institute for Rational-Emotive Therapy.

*_____(1994a). "Rational Emotive Behavior Therapy Approaches to Obsessive-Compulsive Disorder (OCD)." *Journal of Rational-Emotive and Cognitive-Behavior Therapy* 12 (pp. 121–41).

*_____(1994b). *Reason and Emotion in Psychotherapy.* Revised and updated. New York: Birch Lane Press.

*_____(1994c). "The Treatment of Borderline Personalities With Rational-Emotive Behavior Therapy." *Journal of Rational-Emotive and Cognitive-Behavior Therapy* 12 (pp. 101–19).

*_____(1995). "Rational-Emotive Behavior Therapy." In R. Corsini and D. Wedding, eds., *Current Psychotherapies* (pp. 162–96). Itasca, IL: Peacock.

**_____(1996a). *REBT Diminishes Much of the Human Ego.* New York: Albert Ellis Institute.

_____(1996b). "Responses to Criticisms of Rational Emotive Behavior

Therapy (REBT)." *Journal of Rational and Cognitive Behavior Therapy* 14 (pp. 97–121).

*_____(1996c). "Transcript of Demonstration Session II." In W. Dryden, *Learning From Demonstration Sessions* (pp. 91–117). London: Whurr.

**Ellis, A., and Abrams, M. (1994). *How to Cope With a Fatal Illness*. New York: Barricade Books.

**Ellis, A., Abrams, M., and Dengelegi, L. (1992). *The Art and Science of Rational Eating*. New York: Barricade Books.

**Ellis, A., and Becker, I. (1982). *A Guide to Personal Happiness*. North Hollywood, CA: Wilshire Books.

*Ellis, A., and Bernard, M. E., eds., (1985). *Clinical Applications of Rational-Emotive Therapy*. New York: Plenum.

*Ellis, A., and DiGiuseppe, R. (Speakers) (1994). *Dealing With Addictions*. Videotape. New York: Institute for Rational-Emotive Therapy.

**Ellis, A., and DiMattia, D. (1991). *Self-Management: Strategies for Personal Success*. New York: Institute for Rational-Emotive Therapy.

*Ellis, A., and Dryden, W. (1990). *The Essential Albert Ellis*. New York: Springer.

*_____(1991). *A Dialogue With Albert Ellis: Against Dogma*. Philadelphia: Open University Press.

*_____(1997). *The Practice of Rational Emotive Behavior Therapy*. New York: Springer.

Ellis, A., Gordon, J., Neenan, M., and Palmer, S. (1997). *Stress Counseling: A Rational-Emotive Behavior Approach*. London: Cassell. New York: Springer.

*Ellis, A., and Grieger, R. eds. (1986). *Handbook of Rational-Emotive Therapy*, vol. 2. New York: Springer.

**Ellis, A., and Harper, R. A. (1961). *A Guide to Successful Marriage*. North Hollywood, CA: Wilshire Books.

**_____(1997). *A Guide to Rational Living*, 3d revised edition. North Hollywood, CA: Wilshire Books.

**Ellis, A., and Knaus, W. (1977). *Overcoming Procrastination*. New York: New American Library.

**Ellis, A., and Lange, A. (1994). *How to Keep People From Pushing Your Buttons*. New York: Carol Publishing.

*Ellis, A., and Robb, H. (1994). "Acceptance in Rational-Emotive Therapy." In S. C. Hayes, N. S. Jacobson, V. M. Follette, and M. J. Dougher, eds., *Acceptance and Change: Content and Context in Psychotherapy* (pp. 91–102). Reno, NV: Context Press.

*Ellis, A., Sichel, J., Leaf, R. C., and Mass, R. (1989). "Countering Perfectionism in Research on Clinical Practice. I: Surveying Rationality

Changes After a Single Intensive RET Intervention." *Journal of Rational-Emotive and Cognitive-Behavior Therapy* 7 (pp. 197–218).

*Ellis, A., Sichel, J. L., Yeager, R. J., DiMattia, D. J., and DiGiuseppe, R. A. (1989). *Rational-Emotive Couples Therapy*. Needham, MA: Allyn and Bacon.

**Ellis, A., and Velten, E. (1992). *When A A Doesn't Work for You: Rational Steps for Quitting Alcohol*. New York: Barricade Books.

*Engels, G. I., Garnefski, N., and Diekstra, R. F. W. (1993). "Efficacy of Rational-Emotive Therapy: A Quantitative Analysis." *Journal of Consulting and Clinical Psychology* 61 (pp. 1083–90).

**Epictetus (1890). *The Collected Works of Epictetus*. Boston: Little, Brown.

**Epicurus (1994). *Letter on Happiness*. San Francisco: Chronicle Books.

**Epstein, S. (1993). *You're Smarter Than You Think*. New York: Simon & Schuster.

Erikson, Erik. (1969) *Gandhi's Truth*. New York: Norton.

**Fensterheim. H., and Baer, J. (1975). *Don't Say Yes When You Want to Say No*. New York: Dell.

*FitzMaurice, K. (1994). *Introducing the 12 Steps of Emotional Disturbances*. Omaha, NE: Author.

**Foa, E. B., and Wilson, R. (1991). *Stop Obsessing: How to Overcome Your Obsessions and Compulsions*. New York: Bantam.

*Frank, J. D., and Frank, J. B. (1991). *Persuasion and Healing*. Baltimore, MD: Johns Hopkins University Press.

*Frankl, V. (1959). *Man's Search for Meaning*. New York: Pocket Books.

**Franklin, R. (1993). *Overcoming the Myth of Self-Worth*. Appleton, WI: Focus Press.

**Freeman, A., and DeWolfe, R. (1993). *The Ten Dumbest Mistakes Smart People Make and How to Avoid Them*. New York: Harper Perennial.

**Froggatt, W. (1993). *Choose to Be Happy*. New Zealand: Harper-Collins.

*Fromm, E. (1974). *The Anatomy of Human Destructiveness*. Greenwich, CT: Fawcett.

*Gandy, G. L. (1995). *Mental Health Rehabilitation: Disputing Irrational Beliefs*. Springfield, IL: Thomas.

Geen, R., and Stoner, D. (1975). "The Facilitation of Aggression: Evidence Against the Catharsis Hypothesis." *Journal of Personal and Social Psychology* 31 (pp. 721–26).

*Goldfried, M. R., and Davison, G. C. (1994). *Clinical Behavior Therapy*, 3d ed. New York: Holt Rinehart & Winston.

*Grieger, R. M. (1988). "From a Linear to a Contextual Model of the ABCs of RET." In W. Dryden and P. Trower, eds., *Developments in Cognitive Psychotherapy* (pp. 71–105). London: Sage.

**Grieger, R. M., and Woods, P. J. (1993). *The Rational-Emotive Therapy Companion*. Roanoke, VA: Scholars Press.

*Guidano, V. F. (1991). *The Self in Progress*. New York: Guilford.

*Haaga, D. A., and Davison, G. C. (1989). "Outcome Studies of Rational-Emotive Therapy." In M. E. Bernard and R. DiGiuseppe, eds., *Inside Rational-Emotive Therapy* (pp. 155–97). San Diego, CA: Academic Press.

*Hajzler, D., and Bernard, M. E. (1991). "A Review of Rational-Emotive Outcome Studies." *School Psychology Quarterly* 6 (1) (pp. 27–49).

*Haley, J. (1990). *Problem Solving Therapy*. San Francisco: Jossey-Bass.

**Hauck, P. A. (1973). *Overcoming Depression*. Philadelphia: Westminster.

**———(1974). *Overcoming Frustration and Anger*. Philadelphia: Westminster.

**———(1977). *Marriage Is a Loving Business*. Philadelphia: Westminster.

**———(1991). *Overcoming the Rating Game: Beyond Self-Love—Beyond Self-Esteem*. Louisville, KY: Westminster/John Knox.

Helmers, K. F., Posluszny, D. M., and Krantz, D . S. (1994). "Association of Hostility and Coronary Artery Disease: A Review of Studies." In A. W. Siegman and T. W. Smith, eds., *Anger, Hostility and the Heart* (pp. 67–96). Hillsdale, NJ: Lawrence Erlbaum Associates.

Hold, A. (1971). Cited in A. Ellis and J. Gullo, *Murder and Assassination* (pp. 355–56). New York: Lyle Stuart.

*Hollon, S. D., and Beck, A. T. (1994). "Cognitive and Cognitive/Behavioral Therapies." In A. E. Bergin and S. L. Garfield, eds., *Handbook of Psychotherapy and Behavior Change* (pp. 428–66). New York: Wiley.

*Huber, C. H., and Baruth, L. G. (1989). *Rational-Emotive and Systems Family Therapy*. New York: Springer.

*Jacobson, N. S. (1992). "Behavioral Couple Therapy: A New Beginning." *Behavior Therapy* 23 (pp. 491–506).

Jehoda, M. (1961). "What Is Prejudice?" *World Mental Health* 13 (pp. 38–45).

*Johnson, W. (1946). *People in Quandaries*. New York: Harper & Row.

*Johnson, W. R. (1981). *So Desperate the Fight*. New York: Institute for Rational-Emotive Therapy.

Kabit-Zinn, J. (1994). *Wherever You Go There You Are*. New York: Hyperion.

*Kanfer, F. H., and Schefft, B. K. (1988). *Guiding the Process of Therapeutic Change*. New York: Pergamon.

*Kassinove, H., ed. (1995). *Anger Disorders: Definition, Diagnosis, and Treatment*. Washington, DC: Taylor & Francis.

Kassinove, H., Sukhodolsky, D., Tsytsarev, S., and Solovyova, S. (1997). "Self-Reported Anger Episodes in Russia and America." *Journal of Social Behavior and Personality* 12 (1).

*Kelly, G. (1955). *The Psychology of Personal Constructs*. 2 vols. New York: Norton.

King, M. L. (1966, October). "Nonviolence: The Only Road to Freedom." *Ebony* (pp. 27–34).

*Knaus, W. (1974). *Rational-Emotive Education*. New York: Institute for Rational-Emotive Therapy.

———Knaus, W. (1995). *Smart Recovery: A Sensible Primer*. Longmeadow, MA: Author.

*Kopec, A. M., Beal, D., and DiGiuseppe, R. (1994). "Training in RET: Disputational Strategies." *Journal of Rational-Emotive and Cognitive-Behavior Therapy* 12 (pp. 47–60).

*Korzybski, A. (1933). *Science and Sanity*. San Francisco: International Society of General Semantics.

*Kwee, M. G. T. (1982). "Psychotherapy and the Practice of General Semantics." *Methodology and Science* 15 (pp. 236–56).

*———(1991). *Psychotherapy, Meditation, and Health: A Cognitive Behavioral Perspective*. London: East/West Publication.

*Lange, A., and Jakubowski, P. (1976). *Responsible Assertive Behavior*. Champaign, IL: Research Press.

*Lazarus, A. A. (1977). "Toward an Egoless State of Being." In A. Ellis and R. Grieger, eds. *Handbook of Rational-Emotive Therapy*, vol. 1 (pp. 113–16). New York: Springer.

**———(1985). *Marital Myths*. San Luis Obispo, CA: Impact.

*———(1989). *The Practice of Multimodal Therapy*. Baltimore, MD: Johns Hopkins.

**Lazarus, A. A., and Fay, A. (1975). *I Can If I Want To*. New York: Morrow.

**Lazarus, A. A., Lazarus, C., and Fay, A. (1993). *Don't Believe It for a Minute: Forty Toxic Ideas That Are Driving You Crazy*. San Luis Obispo, CA: Impact Publishers.

*Lazarus, R. S., and Folkman, S. (1984). *Stress, Appraisal, and Coping*. New York: Springer.

**Lewinsohn, P., Antonuccio, D., Breckenridge, J., and Teri, L. (1984). *The "Coping With Depression Course."* Eugene, OR: Castalia.

Lewis, W. A., and Butcher, A. M. (1992). "Anger, Catharsis, the Reformulated Frustration-Aggression Hypothesis, and Health Consequences." *Psychotherapy* 23 (3) (pp. 385–92).

*Lipsey, M. W., and Wilson, D. B. (1993). "The Efficacy of Psychological, Educational, and Behavior Treatment: Confirmation from Meta-Analysis." *American Psychologist* 48 (pp. 1181–1209).

**London, T. (1995). *REBT Questions: A Study Guide to the General/Clinical*

Theory, Philosophy, and Techniques of Rational Emotive Behavior Therapy. Chicago: Garfield Press.

**Low, A. A. (1952). *Mental Health Through Will Training*. Boston: Christopher.

*Lyons, L. C., and Woods, P. J. (1991). "The Efficacy of Rational-Emotive Therapy: A Quantitative Review of the Outcome Research." *Clinical Psychology Review* 11 (pp. 357–69).

*Mace, D. (1976). "Marital Intimacy and the Deadly Lover Cycle." *Journal of Marriage and Family Counseling* 2 (pp. 131–37).

Mahoney, M. J. (1991). *Human Change Processes*. New York: Basic Books.

*_____ed. (1995). *Cognitive and Constructive Psychotherapies: Theory, Research and Practice*. New York: Springer.

**Marcus Aurelius. (1890). *Meditations*. Boston: Little, Brown.

*Maultsby, M. C., Jr. (1984). *Rational Behavior Therapy*. Englewood Cliffs, NJ: Prentice-Hall.

McCall, M. W., and Lombardo, M. M. (1983). *Off the Track: Why and How Successful Executives Get Derailed*. (Technical Report No. 21). Greensboro, NC: Center for Creative Leadership.

*McGovern, T. E., and Silverman, M. S. (1984). "A Review of Outcome Studies of Rational-Emotive Therapy From 1977 to 1982." *Journal of Rational-Emotive Therapy* 2 (1) (pp. 7–18).

**McKay, G. D., and Dinkmeyer, D. (1994). *How You Feel Is Up to You*. San Luis Obispo, CA: Impact Publishers.

*McMullin, R. (1986). *Handbook of Cognitive Therapy Techniques*. New York: Norton.

*Meichenbaum, D. (1977). *Cognitive-Behavior Modification*. New York: Plenum.

**Miller, T. (1986). *The Unfair Advantage*. Manlius, NY: Horsesense, Inc.

**Mills, D. (1993). *Overcoming Self-Esteem*. New York: Institute for Rational-Emotive Therapy.

*Muran, J. C. (1991). "A Reformulation of the ABC Model in Cognitive Psychotherapies: Implications for Assessment and Treatment." *Clinical Psychology Review* 11 (pp. 399–418).

**Nottingham, E. (1992). *It's Not as Bad as It Seems: A Thinking Approach to Happiness*. Memphis, TN: Castle Books.

*Novaco, R. W. (1994, August). *Psychological Treatment of Anger and Aggression: Successful Achievement and Refractory Impediments*. Paper presented at the Annual Meeting of the American Psychological Association, Los Angeles, CA.

Novello, A., Shosky, S., and Froehlke, R. (1992). "From the Surgeon General U. S. Public Health Service: A Medical Response to Violence."

Journal of the American Medical Association 267 (22) (p. 3007).

**Nye, B. (1993). *Understanding and Managing Your Anger and Aggression*. Federal Way, WA: BCA Publishing.

Olsen, K. (1975). *The Art of Hanging Loose*. Greenwich, CT: Fawcett.

*Palmer, S., and Dryden, W. (1996). *Stress Management and Counseling*. London and New York: Cassell.

*Palmer, S., Dryden, W., Ellis, A., and Yapp, R. (1995). *Rational Interviews*. London: Centre for Rational Emotive Behavior Therapy.

*Palmer, S., and Ellis, A. (1994). "In the Counselor's Chair." *The Rational Emotive Therapist* 2 (1) (pp. 6–15). From *Counseling Journal* 4 (pp. 171–74). (1993).

Peters, H. (1970). "The Education of the Emotions." In M. Arnold, ed. *Feelings and Emotions*. New York: Academic Press (pp. 187–203).

*Phadke, K. M. (1982). "Some Innovations in RET Theory and Practice." *Rational Living* 17 (2) (pp. 25–30).

*Pietsch. W. V. (1993). *The Serenity Prayer*. San Francisco: Harper San Francisco.

*Prochaska, J. O., DiClemente, C. C., and Norcross, J. C. (1992). "In Search of How People Change: Applications to Addictive Behaviors." *American Psychologist* 47 (pp. 1102–14).

**Robin, M. W., and Balter, R. (1995). *Performance Anxiety*. Holbrook, MA: Adams.

*Rorer, L. G. (1989). "Rational-Emotive Theory: I. An Integrated Psychological and Philosophic Basis. II. Explication and Evaluation." *Cognitive Therapy and Research* 13 (pp. 475–92, 531–48).

Rothenberg, A. (1971) "On Anger." *American Journal of Psychiatry* 128 (pp. 454–60).

**Russell, B. (1950). *The Conquest of Happiness*. New York: New American Library.

Sapolsky, R. M. (1994). *Why Zebras Don't Get Ulcers: A Guide to Stress, Stress-Related Diseases and Coping*. New York: W. H. Freeman and Company.

**Sarmiento, R. F. (1993). *Reality Check: Twenty Questions to Screw Your Head on Straight*. Houston, TX: Bunker Hill Press.

**Seligman, M. E. P. (1991). *Learned Optimism*. New York: Knopf.

**Seligman, M. E. P., with Revich, K., Jaycox, L., and Gillham, J. (1995). *The Optimistic Child*. New York: Houghton Mifflin.

Seneca, L. A. (1963). "On Anger." In J. W. Basore, trans., *Moral Essays*. Cambridge, MA: Harvard University Press.

**Sichel, J., and Ellis, A. (1984). *REBT Self-Help Form*. New York: Institute for Rational- Emotive Therapy.

Siegman, A. W. (1994). "Cardiovascular Consequences of Expressing and Repressing Anger." In A. Siegman and T. Smith, eds., *Anger, Hostility*, *and the Heart*. Hillsdale, NJ: Lawrence Erlbaum Associates.

*Silverman, M. S., McCarthy, M., and McGovern, T. (1992). "A Review of Outcome Studies of Rational-Emotive Therapy From 1982–1989." *Journal of Rational-Emotive and Cognitive-Behavior Therapy* 10 (3) (pp. 111–86).

**Simon, J. L. (1993). *Good Mood*. LaSalle, IL: Open Court.

*Smith, M. L., and Glass, G. V. (1977). "Meta-Analysis of Psychotherapy Outcome Studies." *American Psychologist* 32 (pp. 752–60).

*Stanton, H. E. (1989). "Hypnosis and Rational-Emotive Therapy—A De-stressing Combination." *International Journal of Clinical and Experimental Hypnosis* 37 (pp. 95–99).

Straus, M. A., and Gelles, R. J. (1992). "How Violent Are American Families? Estimates From the National Family Violence Resurvey and Other Surveys." In M. A. Straus and R. J. Gelles, eds. *Physical Violence in American Families* (pp. 95–109). New Brunswick, NJ: Transaction Publishers.

**Tate, P. (1993). *Alcohol: How to Give It Up and Be Glad You Did*. Altamonte Springs, FL: Rational Self-Help Press.

Travis, C. (1989). *Anger: The Misunderstood Emotion*, 2d ed. New York: Touchstone.

Thompson, W. I. (1975, July 1). "We Become What We Hate." *New York Times* (p. E11).

*Tillich, P. (1953). *The Courage to Be*. New York: Oxford.

**Trimpey, J. (1989). *Rational Recovery From Alcoholism: The Small Book*. New York: Delacorte.

United States Advisory Board on Child Abuse and Neglect. (1995). *A Nation's Shame: Fatal Child Abuse and Neglect in the United States*. Washington, DC: U.S. Government Printing Office.

United States Bureau of the Census. (1995). *Statistical Abstract of the United States*. Washington, DC: U.S. Government Printing Office.

United States Department of Justice. (1995). *Uniform Crime Reports*. Washington, DC: U.S. Government Printing Office.

**Velten, E. (Speaker) (1987). *How to Be Unhappy at Work*. Cassette recording. New York: Institute for Rational-Emotive Therapy.

*Vernon, A. (1989). *Thinking, Feeling, Behaving: An Emotional Education Curriculum for Children*. Champaign, IL: Research Press.

*Walen, S., DiGiuseppe, R., and Dryden, W. (1992). *A Practitioner's Guide to Rational-Emotive Therapy*. New York: Oxford University Press.

**Walter, M. (1994). *Personal Resilience*. Kanata, Ontario, Canada: Resilience Training International.

*Warga, C. (1988). "Profile of Psychologist Albert Ellis." *Psychology Today* September (pp. 18–33). Rev. ed., New York: Institute for Rational-

Emotive Therapy, 1989.

*Warren, R., and Zgourides, G. D. (1991). *Anxiety Disorders: A Rational-Emotive Perspective*. Des Moines, IA: Longwood Division Allyn & Bacon.

**Watson, D., and Tharp, R. (1993). *Self-Directed Behavior*, 6th ed. Pacific Grove, CA: Brooks/Cole.

*Weinrach, S. G. (1980). "Unconventional Therapist: Albert Ellis." *Personnel and Guidance Journal* 59 (pp. 152–60).

*_____(1995). "Rational Emotive Behavior Therapy: A Tough-Minded Therapy for a Tender-Minded Profession." *Journal of Counseling and Development* 73 (pp. 296–300). Also in W. Dryden, ed., *Rational-Emotive Behavior Therapy: A Reader* (pp. 303–12). London: Sage.

*Wiener, D. (1988). *Albert Ellis: Passionate Skeptic*. New York: Praeger.

*Wolfe, J. L. (1977). *Assertiveness Training for Women*. Cassette recording. New York: BMA Audio Cassettes.

*_____(Speaker) (1980). *Woman—Assert Yourself*. Cassette recording. New York: Institute for Rational-Emotive Therapy.

**_____(1992). *What to Do When He Has a Headache*. New York: Hyperion.

**_____(1993). *How Not to Give Yourself a Headache When Your Partner Isn't Acting the Way You'd Like*. New York: Institute for Rational-Emotive Therapy.

**_____(Speaker) (1993). "Overcoming Low Frustration Tolerance." Videocassette. New York: Institute for Rational-Emotive Therapy.

*Wolfe, J. L., and Naimark, H. (1991). "Psychological Messages and Social Context. Strategies for Increasing RET's Effectiveness With Women." In M. Bernard, ed., *Using Rational-Emotive Therapy Effectively*. New York: Plenum.

**Woods, P. J. (1990). *Controlling Your Smoking: A Comprehensive Set of Strategies for Smoking Reduction*. Roanoke, VA: Scholars Press.

*_____(1993). "Building Positive Self-Regard." In M. E. Bernard and J. L. Wolfe, eds., *The RET Resource Book for Practitioners* (pp. 158–61).

*Yankura, J., and Dryden, W. (1990). *Doing RET: Albert Ellis in Action*. New York: Springer.

*_____(1994). *Albert Ellis*. Thousand Oaks, CA: Sage.

**Young, H. S. (1974). *A Rational Counseling Primer*. New York: Institute for Rational-Emotive Therapy.

Index

abreactive therapies, 19–21, 29, 70–71
absurdity and irrational beliefs, 111–14
abuse
    child, 10, 131
    spousal, 9–10
acceptance, 61, 62–64, 144–50
acting way out of anger, 72–91
actions and people, separation of. See
    overgeneralization
Activating Experience (A). See
    Adversity
activism, 132–33
Adler, Alfred, 129
Adversity (A), 60
    awfulizing about, 43
    Beliefs about (B), 31, 32
    Consequences and (C), 31–32
    definition of, 31–32
aggression
    anger sparks, 9–11
    assertion versus, 68–69, 78–79,
        82–83, 133
    biological elements of, 137
    inherited, 48
Alberti, Robert E., 81, 82
alcohol abuse, 135–36
all or nothingism, 43
anxiety, 74–75
    Irrational Beliefs (IBs) and, 41–42,
        50, 139–40
approval musts, 45
Arendt, Hannah, 132
assertion training, 68–69, 78–85
assertiveness
    acting assertive, 83–84
    aggression versus, 68–69, 78–79,
        82–83, 133
    degrees of, 84–85
atherosclerosis, 12
attitudes toward anger, 39–40

attribution theory, 134–35
avoidance of feelings, 21–22, 74
awfulizing, 43, 52, 53, 54, 56

Bach, George, 81, 118
Baer, Jean, 148
Bandura, Albert, 73, 125
bargaining assertiveness, 84–85
Barton, Robert, 88
Behavioral Effect (E), 61
behavioral exercises, 74–91
behavioral methods of reducing anger,
    62, 72–91, 122–23
behavioral Consequence (C). See
    emotional Consequence
behavior-reversal techniques, 69
Belief Systems (B), 31–32. See also
    Irrational Beliefs; Rational Beliefs
    categories of, 33–34
    changing, 35–36, 39–40, 48
    definition of, 31, 32
Bell, Paul, 88
biological roots of aggression, 137
Bird, Lois, 80
blood pressure, 12
Boorstin, Daniel J., 130
Burns, David, 133

Cannon, Walter, 11
can't-stand-it-itis, 43, 56–57
cathartic therapies, 19–20, 69
causes of anger, 30–32
children
    abuse of, 10, 131
    punishment of, 47–48
Cognitive Behavior Therapy (CBT),
    28, 30
cognitive Effect (E), 61
cognitive restructuring exercises,
    89–90

competition, 142–43
conditioning, 87–88
confrontation exercises, 80–81
constructive activities and reducing anger, 87
Constructive Beliefs (RBs). *See* Rational Beliefs
contingency management, 76–77
contracts, 76–77
coping procedures, 89
coping statements, 100–102
coronary heart disease, 12–13
    venting anger and, 19–20
costs of anger, 3–17
    aggression and, 9–11
    difficult situations, 8–9
    heart disease, 11–13
    personal distress, 13–16
    to personal relationships, 3–5
    to work relationships, 5–8
courage exercises, 80–81
coworker relationships, 5–8
creativity, 40

damnation, 43
Danysh, Joseph, 108, 109–10
Davis, Martha Penn, 87
debating Irrational Beliefs (IBs), 51–52, 56–58
Deffenbacher, Jerry, 90, 92, 114
Denenberg, Victor, 87–88
depression, 14–15, 41–42
Destructive Beliefs (IBs). *See* Irrational Beliefs
detecting Irrational Beliefs (IBs), 51
difficult situations, 8–9, 25–26
    relaxation techniques under, 97–100
Disputing (D), 32, 36, 49–50, 51–54, 61, 145–46
    exercises in, 103–8
Disputing Irrational Beliefs (DIBs), 103–8
distraction measures against anger, 88–89
distress, 13–16
dogmatism, overcoming, 130
drinking, 135–36
drug abuse, 135–36

embarrassment and anger, 15, 67–68

Emmons, Michael E., 81, 82
emotional Consequence (C), 30–35
    Adversity and (A), 30–32
    Beliefs influence (B), 31–32
    definition of, 30–31
    negative feelings and, 33
emotional distress, 13–16
emotive methods for reducing anger, 35, 62–71
Erikson, Erik, 139
esteem, 59–60
events, reacting to, 25–26
exercises for reducing anger
    behavioral, 74–91
    cognitive restructuring, 89–90
    Disputing Irrational Beliefs, 103–8
    emotive, 62–71
expression of anger, 19–21, 29, 70–71

failure exercises, 80
fallibility, human, 136–37
family violence, 9–10
Fay, Allen, 82
feeling out of anger, 62–71
Fensterheim, Herbert, 148
"fight of flight" response, 11–12
firm kindness, 148
forgiveness, 29, 136–37
Frankl, Viktor, 111
free expression of anger, 19–21, 29, 70–71
Freud, Sigmund, 19, 88, 129. *See also* psychoanalytic technique
Fromm, Erich, 128
frustration, 125–27
    homework assignments for, 75–76
    Irrational Beliefs (IBs) and, 42–43
    low frustration tolerance (LFT), 57, 75
    tolerance of, 127–28

Gandhi, Mahatma, 139
"Garland of Rational Songs, A," 116–18
genetic factors, 48, 87–88
Gestalt therapy, 69
Goldberg, Herb, 81
grandiosity, 128–30
Green, Russell, 134
guilt, 15

Hare, Rachel, 113–14
harm of anger. *See* costs of anger
Harper, Robert A., 121
hatred, 131–32, 139–40
Hauck, Paul A., 132, 150
Hayakawa, S. I., 109
healthy negative feelings, 32, 54, 64–65, 67
heart disease, 11–13
    venting anger and, 19–20
Hewes, David D., 83–84
high blood pressure, 12
Hold, Anatol, 136–37
homework assignments for anger. *See* exercises
hostile attributional bias, 133–35
hostility. *See also* aggression
    exposure to, 87
    reviewing results of, 125–27
    shame-attacking exercises and, 68
humanistic values, 140–41
humor, 114–18

I-can't-stand-it-itis, 43, 56–57
imagery, 97–100
I-messages and assertion, 83–84
inadequacy, feelings of, 135
indignation, 137–39, 150
inherited aggressive tendency, 48
injustice, 132
insight
    psychoanalytic, 23–25, 39, 47–48
    REBT, 39–40, 47–50
integrative therapy, REBT as, 90
intimate relations, 118
Irrational Beliefs (IBs), 32, 33–38
    absurdity and, 111–14
    anxiety and, 41–42, 50, 139–40
    debating of, 51–52, 56–58
    definition of, 32, 33
    Disputing, 32, 36, 49–50, 51–54, 145–46
    locating, 34, 40, 41
    main, 34–35, 36–37, 40–41, 51–52
    musturbatory headings of, 40, 42–44
    repetition of, 48–49
    uprooting, 35–36, 41–42, 56
    variations on, 44–46
irrational musts, 45–46, 57–58

I-statements, 146–47
"I Wish I Were Not Crazy," 117

Jahoda, Marie, 131
Jakubowski, Patricia, 83
James, William, 88
jocularity, 114–18
Johnson, Wendell, 109

Kassinove, Howard, 89, 92
King, Martin Luther, Jr., 139
Korzybski, Alfred, 58, 109

Lange, Arthur, 83
Lasch, Christopher, 139
laughing at yourself, 114–18
Lazarus, Arnold, 82, 84
letting out anger, 19–21, 29, 70–71
life conditions, irrational musts about, 45–46
"Love Me, Love Me, Only Me!", 117–18
low frustration tolerance (LFT), 57, 75

Mace, David, 118, 120
marital relations, 118
Maultsby, Maxie C., Jr., 64
Meichenbaum, Donald, 89–90
models for behavior, 85–87
Moreno, J. L., 69
muscle relaxation, 92–96
musturbation and musts, 40, 42–44, 45–46, 56, 57–58
myths about dealing with anger, 18–26
    free expression, 19–21
    getting what you want, 22–23
    insight into your past, 23–25
    outside events, 25–26
    time out, 21–22

narcissism, 128–30
negative feelings
    distinguishing, 53–54
    healthy, 32, 54, 64–65, 67
    unhealthy, 32, 42, 54, 61
New Philosophy (E), 61
nonviolence, 138–39
Novaco, Raymond, 89–90
Nye, Bud, 150

Olsen, Ken, 140

operant conditioning, 76–77
others
　　hatred of, 131–32
　　irrational musts about, 45, 57–58
　　pain of, 141
outside events, 25–26
overgeneralization, 43, 58, 109–11

pain of others, 141
paradoxical intention, 111–14
past, insights into, 23–25, 39, 47–48
penalties and rewards, 76–78
"Perfect Rationality," 116–17
Perls, Fritz, 69
personal distress, 13–16
Peters, H., 129
Phadke, Kishor, 51
physical changes and anger, 12, 20
pleasurable emotions, 66–67
political violence, 131
positive emotions, 66–67
positive reinforcement, 76–77
practical results of anger, 125–27
prejudice, 131–32
problem-solving procedures, 89
progressive muscle relaxation (PMR),
　　92–96
psychoanalytic techniques
　　failure of, 23–25
　　insight, 23–35, 39, 47–48
put-downs, 147–49

rage, 7, 15–16, 133
　　physical changes and, 12
　　reduction techniques, 64–66
　　venting of, 19–21
Ramsay, R. W., 66
rational anger, 59–60
Rational Beliefs (RBs), 32, 33–83
　　definition of, 33–34
　　locating, 34, 40, 41
rational coping statements, 100–102
Rational Emotive Behavior Therapy
　　(REBT), x, 27–32
　　behavioral methods of, 62, 72–91,
　　　122–23
　　Disputing Irrational Beliefs method,
　　　103–8
　　emotive methods of, 35, 62–71
　　insights of, 39–40, 47–50

principles of, 27–32, 33–38
Self-Help Form, 54–55, 153–57
Rational Emotive Imagery (REI),
　　64–67
referenting technique, 108–11
reinforcement, 76–777
relationships
　　close, reducing anger in, 118–22
　　enhancing your, 141–42
　　personal, 3–5
　　work, 5–8
relaxation techniques, 88, 92–101
　　under difficult circumstances,
　　　97–100
　　progressive muscle relaxation, 92–96
　　short version, 96–97
religious warfare, 131
reprisal, 130–31
reward and punishment, 76–77
rewards and anger, 21–22
ridicule, 5–6
righteous indignation, 137–39, 150
risk-taking exercises, 67, 68, 79–80, 85
Rochlin, Gregory, 128, 129
Rogers, Carl, 122
role-playing, 69–70, 81
Roosevelt, Eleanor, 47
Rothenberg, Allen, 19
Russell, George William, 132

Sapolsky, Robert, 12
sarcasm, 148–49
self-acceptance, 61, 62–64, 149
self-assertion, 68–69, 78–83
self-blaming, 29
self-condemnation, 59–60
self-control procedures, 76–77
self-damnation, 43, 78
self-defeating demands and behaviors,
　　45–46, 76–77
self-defense, 86
self-efficacy, 73
self-esteem, 59–60, 129
self-hatred, 59–60, 139–40
Self-Help Form, 54–55, 153–57
self-interest, 140–41
semantic overgeneralization, 108–11
Seneca, 8
shame-attacking exercises, 67–68, 80
Siegman, Aaron, 19–20

Skinner, B. F., 76, 125
Smaby, Marlowe H., 84
spousal abuse, 9–10
Stonner, David, 134
stubbornness, dealing with, 112–14
Sturek, Joseph, 137
sublimation, 88
substance abuse, 135–36

Tamminen, Armas W., 84
temper tantrums, 113–14, 124
tension, progressive muscle relaxation
    and, 92–96
Thompson, William Irwin, 132
"time-out" strategies, 21–22
training courses for reducing anger,
    143
turning the other cheek, 29, 136–37

unassertiveness, 68–69, 82
unconditional acceptance, 62–64

unfairness. *See* injustice
unhealthy negative feelings, 32, 42, 54,
    61

values
    experiences given, 32
    humanistic, 140–41
venting anger, 19–21, 29, 70–71
violence, 9–10

Wachtel, Andrew S., 87
"Whine, Whine, Whine," 116
Wolfe, Janet L., 83, 133
work relationships, 5–8
workshops for reducing anger, 143

you-messages and assertion, 83–84
you-statements, 146

Zarrow, M. J., 87–88
Zinberg, Norman, 88

About the Authors

Albert Ellis has M.A. and Ph.D. degrees in clinical psychology from Columbia University. He is the founder of Rational Emotive Behavior Therapy (REBT), the pioneering form of the modern Cognitive Behavior therapies. He is the president of the Albert Ellis Institute in New York, where he practices individual and group psychotherapy, supervises and trains psychotherapists, and presents many talks and workshops at the Institute and throughout the world. He has published over seven hundred articles and more than sixty books on psychotherapy, marital and family therapy, and sex therapy.

Raymond Chip Tafrate earned his bachelor's degree from the University of Vermont and his M.A and Ph.D. degrees in clinical psychology from Hofstra University. A fellow of the Albert Ellis Institute for Rational Emotive Behavior therapy and a licensed psychologist in New York, Dr. Tafrate currently serves as an assistant professor in the sociology and criminal justice department at Central Connecticut State University. He conducts research on the assessment, diagnosis, and treatment of people with anger problems, and his work in this area has been published in several scientific journals and books and been presented at many professional conferences in the United States and abroad.